KV-745-157

'Litt's weird, wonderful and very witty stories ... will make you laugh and occasionally shudder, but, most of all, they'll make you think'

*Cosmopolitan*

'There are plenty of nods to e-mail, Bjork albums and Wagamama, but unlike the predictably label-conscious, metropolitan sensibility afflicting so many young (male) writers who have a kind of oedipal thing with Martin Amis, Toby Litt has a truly satirical sense of fun: forget the sententious-sounding Capitalism of the title, just think Adventures'

*Independent*

'Hark at Lord Byron!'

*Loaded*

'A genuinely individual talent [with] a positive relish for dealing with the most contemporary aspects of the modern world. The stories bristle with references to computer technology, advertising, films and current designer labels, and there is undoubtedly an exhilaration involved in seeing these things cross over into fiction'

*Scotsman*

'In the world of three-minute wonders, premature publishers and out-and-out firers of blanks which is the current Literary Lad scene, Toby Litt is that once-in-a-lifetime blind date who goes on to give you the time of your life. If *Adventures in Capitalism* doesn't make you want to have him or be him, you're dead'

Julie Burchill

'Toby Litt is that rare writer whose work can justify the boldest claims about his talent'

*G•Spot*

'His take on life is very strange, but very charming too ... He is Britain's answer to Douglas Coupland'

Alain de Botton

'The cerebral amongst us will find the book's under-lying concerns of post-modern identity and paranoia absorbing, the rest of us can revel in the cultishness of its references and wistfully sigh for the days when we argued whether VHS, Picturedisc or Betamax was best'

*The Punter*

'Polished and pointless'

*The Times*

'These short, unsettling stories are not po-faced or pinko; they are surreal journeys beneath the surface of our consumer lives'

*Observer*

'Approaches English identity as being nothing more than a hotchpotch of brand images, pop culture and absolute amorality. The closing story, a dream about Foucault, is one of the best I have read this year'

*Harpers & Queen*

'This diverse, accomplished mind-meld of eagerly readable shorts stands as a tantalising tribute to a writer on the edge of greater, grander things. And it's only a début. Christ!'

*Comedy Review*

'He has invented a fresh, contemporary style – it will sing in the ears of this generation'

Malcolm Bradbury

'Extremely modern, funny, disturbing and, of course, about the state of our culture right now'

Nigel Williams

'Litt has conjured up a book of its time. His future is assured'

*Literary Review*

# Adventures in Capitalism

Toby Litt was born in 1968.
He grew up in Ampthill, Bedfordshire.
He was educated in Oxford and East Anglia.
From 1990 to 1993 he lived in Prague.
*Adventures in Capitalism* is his first book.

# Adventures in Capitalism

## TOBY LITT

Minerva

**A Minerva Paperback**
ADVENTURES IN CAPITALISM

Versions of the following stories have appeared in the following places:
'It Could Have Been Me and It Was' in *Concrete*, and in
*Class Work* (Sceptre), along with 'Mr Kipling', 'Please Use a Basket'
and 'Cosmetic'; 'Moriarty' in *Harlequinned*; 'Z-ward, Bojo, Kenneth and
the Betamax Boy' in *Ambit*; and 'Flies II', in
*That Dangerous Supplement*, and in *Concrete*.

The author and publishers gratefully acknowledge permission
to reprint from *The Archaeology of Knowledge* and *The Order of Things*
by Michel Foucault, trans. Alan Sheridan, Tavistock Publications, from
*The Selected Poetry of Ranier Maria Rilke*, trans. Stephen Mitchell, Picador
and from the Wagamama opinionnaire.

'Lost in the Supermarket' words and music by Joe Strummer and
Mick Jones © 1979, reproduced by permission of Nineden Ltd/EMI
Virgin Music Ltd, London WC2H OEA. 'Speedboat' words and music
by Lloyd Cole © 1984, reproduced by permission of EMI Songs Ltd,
London WC2H OEA.

The author would like to thank Malcolm Bradbury, Russell Celyn Jones,
Rob Ritchie, Roger Sales, Jon Cook, Vic Sage; Mic Cheetham,
Neil Taylor; Jacqui Lofthouse, David Lewis, Harriet Braun;
Tom Guest, Richard Beard; Virginia Little; Jean Fielder, Anne Lester.

The author would also like to thank the Sir Richard Stapley Educational
Trust and the Curtis Brown Literary Agency.

First published in Great Britain 1996
by Martin Secker & Warburg Ltd
This Minerva edition published 1997
by Mandarin Paperbacks
an imprint of Reed International Books Ltd
Michelin House, 81 Fulham Road, London SW3 6RB
and Auckland, Melbourne, Singapore and Toronto
www.minervabooks.com

Copyright © 1996 by Toby Litt
The author has asserted his moral rights

A CIP catalogue record for this title
is available from the British Library
ISBN 0 7493 8627 4

Typeset in Bembo
Printed and bound in Great Britain
by Cox & Wyman Ltd, Reading, Berkshire

This book is sold subject to the condition that it shall not, by way of
trade or otherwise, be lent, resold, hired out, or otherwise circulated
without the publisher's prior consent in any form of binding or cover
other than that in which it is published and without a similar condition
including this condition being imposed on the subsequent purchaser.

If the world be promiscuously described...

Samuel Johnson,
*The Rambler*, IV


I'm all lost in the supermarket
I can no longer shop happily
I came in here for that special offer
Guaranteed personality

The Clash,
*Lost in the Supermarket*

# Early Capitalism:

# Late Capitalism:

# Early
# Capitalism

# It Could Have Been Me
# and It Was

After I won the Lottery and jacked in my job at the Lab, I decided, in a spirit of scientific enquiry, to spend a year and a day believing everything the ads told me. *Coke* was *It* and *Pepsi* was *The Choice of a New Generation*. (I was 32 and so wasn't really sure if that meant me.) 'A Year in Fairyland,' I called it, 'The Place Where All Your Dreams Come True'. They'd been telling you (me) from since before you (I) were (was) born that if you (I) just did exactly what they said, you (I) would become 'The New You' ('Me'), so I (on your behalf) decided to obey them (Them).

|  Before:  |  After:  |
|:---:|:---:|
|  |  |
| (Eugh!) | (Phwoar!) |

At the end of the Fairytale Year, I would judge whether I was substantially any happier than I would have been at the end of Just Another Year. Somehow, I doubted it.

Almost immediately, because I live in London, travel by
tube and because it was summer, I got *Heatbusters* to
fit some air conditioning in my flat. 'Phew! Thanks
*Heatbusters*. We needed that.' I drank *Grolsch* and joined
*Dateline*. I *too* could find love. My first date, Lauren,
who worked in qualitative Pharmaceutical Market
Research in Putney, was lovely. But I drank so much
*Grolsch* during the first half of the evening that, during
the second, I metamorphosed into *The Human Whoopee
Cushion*. Lauren told me that a man with my unfortu-
nate problem should seek medical help. But as Lauren
wasn't an ad, I didn't believe her. You see, I'd also decided, about two weeks in, that I'd have to stop believing
people. So when my mother phoned up and said 'Hello,'
I didn't believe her; I said, 'Who are you?' and she said,
'Brian, I'm your mother,' and I said, 'No you're not,' and
put the phone down. This continued for several days
until I managed to buy a new flat. I informed *Dateline* of
my change of address but not the crazed woman
pretending to be my mother. My next two *Dateline* dates
were disastrous: I fell in love with both of them. I'd had
to. If the ad said I *too* could find love through *Dateline*,
then I could. Maria worked for a company that supplied
*VoiceMail*. I soon had *VoiceMail*. Mandy worked as a
receptionist in a Harley Street practice. I soon had no
appendix. In the meantime, of course, I was spotting
other ads in which I couldn't not believe. I bought loads
of stuff. One Friday evening I sat down to watch
*Eurotrash* and the next day I had to go out and buy a Fiat
*Punto*, two Renault *Clios*, a Volkswagen *Polo*, a Citröen
*Xantia*, some *Monster Munch*, *Crunchy Nut Cornflakes*,

a Cadbury's *Twirl* and a pack of Wrigley's *Spearmint Gum*, Andrews *Antacid Indigestion Tablets* (which came in quite handy after I'd eaten the *Monster Munch*), Colgate *Bicarbonate of Soda Toothpaste* (which overcame the ill-effects of the chewing gum), a large box of *Tampax* tampons and a pack of *Energizer* batteries. I had breakfast at Burger King, where a *Whopper* was definitely on the menu, and lunch at McDonald's, where the *Egg McMuffin* was not to be avoided. I also made enquiries about the issue of *PowerGen* shares, took out several *Personal Pension Plans*, opened an account at the *Cooperative Bank* and joined both *WeightWatchers* and the *Territorial Army*. On the next day, Sunday, I bought the *Sunday Telegraph*, which necessitated a further glut of purchases, the most embarrassing of which was the full set of *Birds of the British Isles Heirloom Thimbles*. At this point I almost gave the whole thing up. One evening, when I was out at *WeightWatchers*, Mandy accidentally heard the message that Maria had left on the *VoiceMail*. Maria was thanking me for the *Commitment Ring* I had just sent over to her via *UPS*. That got rid of Mandy. Unfortunately, Maria had left her parents' number in her message (she had gone down to Devon to ask their permission to marry me). Mandy called them up, told them everything, and that got rid of Maria. I lost 10lbs in two weeks, mainly thanks to the *Territorial Army*. The next three dates that *Dateline* sent along were Teresa, a Bicycle Courier who really wanted to be a Nun, Maxine, a Dental Hygienist who was a Transsexual and Sarah, a Nun who couldn't decide whether to become a Bicycle Courier or a Transsexual. I suggested she give Dental Hygiene a try.

My life became busier and busier. As well as all the *Dateline* business, there was the Culture (a hundred must-see and unmissable films, plays and exhibitions), the Investments (*PEPS* and *High Interest Savings Accounts*), the Insurance Policies (*Life, Health, Car, Home*), the Cigarettes (*Silk Cut, Marlboro, Embassy Mild, Benson and Hedges*) and the Properties (Soho Loft, Surrey Tudor, Scottish Castle, Slough Repossession). I was soon skipping *WeightWatchers* meetings and trying to forget I'd ever joined the *Territorials*. I started to wear dark glasses and to walk round looking at my feet, which was cheating, I know. But something big was coming up. Sooner or later, I realized, I would have to stop deceiving myself. I was being hugely inconsistent. I had to get away. I needed a break. I needed a holiday. The *Territorials*, who had started leaving frankly abusive messages on my *VoiceMail*, would have to go stuff. Florida. EuroDisney. Israel. Dublin. Malta. The whole world competed for my body and my cash. In the end, I decided to go out the next morning and obey the first travel advert I saw. I slept badly, dreaming of the thousand places I might have to visit: I arrived in *Pontins* in Welshpool, took a daytrip to the Wailing Wall, got lost in the Galapagos, was mugged in Central Park and finished with some Après-Ski. In the morning I got up, drew the curtains and immediately saw a very scrappy ad on the side of a double-decker bus. It was for Beijing, so to Beijing I went – although I missed several flights on my slow and gradually more and more overladen trip through Heathrow. By the time I found *Air China* Check In, I had stocked up on perfumes and cameras

and extra luggage and towels and novels and the newspapers. They wouldn't allow most of it on the plane, so
I had it posted back to Surrey. It could rot on the lawn.
During the flight I was able to really relax for the first
time in months, though I did feel obliged to get pissed-
up on the *Duty Frees*. You may think me stupid, but it
was only when I arrived in Beijing and stepped out of
the airport that I realized I wasn't able to understand a
single one of the many ads I saw. *Hotel* was the only
word I could decipher. Going back into the airport
would be an act of conscious will. I would be deliberately overriding my ad-obedience, which intended me
to have a holiday in Beijing. All I could do now, therefore, was have a holiday in Beijing. I checked in to my
*Hotel* and started buying things, mainly cans of *Coke*. For
a day or two I tried to decide whether learning
Mandarin would also be a disobedience. I decided it
would. I had six months left in China, then. And after
that, who knows? The *Territorials* would probably have
me Court Marshalled the moment I set foot in Blighty.
And as for *WeightWatchers*, I hardly dared think. There
was nothing else to do. I was stuck. One day I took a
walk away from the *Hotel*, hoping that I would see an ad,
any ad, telling me to go on holiday in Surrey
or London or even just England. There was nothing. Deng
Xiaoping. Televisions. Smiling faces eating rice.
I carried on walking. Wide pale streets full of people riding
bicycles. I was lost. I couldn't go back to the same *Hotel* as
before unless I got lucky and saw an ad for it. But I never
did. My luggage, including my dictionary, faded behind
me as I was pinballed around from foreign *Hotel* to foreign

*Hotel.* Some law of chaos led me gradually north, out of the city. A month had passed. I was a different, bearded, shabby, raving man. I had started to have dreams in which I was a *Monster Munch* monster. I lost my passport, somehow or other, but, thank God, not my *American Express Card*. I found myself in a *Hotel* from which I seemed unable to reach any other *Hotels*. I waited in the lobby for days, hoping for a copy of a foreign newspaper or magazine. Anything. Even *Time Out* would have done. If I had read *Time Out*, I would have had to enroll at the *American College* and to do that I would have had to travel to Marylebone or Malibu or somewhere. But nothing happened to help me. I put the 10 lbs back on, plus. Two months passed and then the woman claiming to be my mother arrived. I couldn't explain to her that I still had three months of my experiment left. She wouldn't have understood. Mothers, true or false, never do. But, bless her, whoever she was, she had a crappy novel with her and in that crappy novel was a complimentary bookmark. By taking out a year's subscription for the *Reader's Digest* (unavailable, as yet, in China), I was able to maintain my pride and consistency. Just. I returned to England with my pseudo-mother, looking forward to receiving my free *Clock Radio*. When we arrived in Heathrow, there was something of an incident. Here, in the Clinic, with a fortnight to go, they have learnt to prevent my escape bids by forbidding me television, newspapers, magazines and any glimpse of buses or taxis. Instead, Doctor Chandra lends me copies of the *Autograph Edition* of the *Complete Works of Charles Dickens*. Every time I finish one, he gives me the next. I am currently reading *Bleak House*.

# Moriarty

Holmes had been pursuing Moriarty for almost three decades. (These, you must know, were not their real names and a decade, as far as they were concerned, lasted about five days.)

Holmes, like her pseudonymsake, was tenacious, melancholic and inspired; Moriarty, like his, was logical and depraved and always evanescent. They were both fifteen.

Holmes first saw Moriarty in the cornfield behind her house. It was three in the morning, August, and there was the fullest of full moons. Moriarty was gliding along one of the parallel furrows left in the waist-high corn by the tractor's wheels. In the pale cinematic of the moonlight, the corn looked like snow.

Moriarty had no legs.

He was like a mediaeval ghost, still walking along at the ground level of its day.

Holmes, who had been standing naked at the bedroom window, dropped a light dress onto herself.

She carried her plimsolls through the house, only putting them on when she'd crossed the lawn.

The grass lisped coolly between her toes.

By the time Holmes caught sight of him again, Moriarty had reached the edge of the pond.

Holmes could hear Moriarty humming or singing or chanting, she couldn't tell which. She drew nearer, positioning herself behind the trunk of The Kissing Tree.

Above them, the moon was besotted with black clouds. The wind blowing past smelt warmly of cotton sheets. There would be a dry thunderstorm before morning.

Moriarty cross-armed his sweater off over his head, heeled himself out of his shoes and palmed down his trousers. Holmes, still watching, plucked away her dress.

Moriarty moved forward into the pond, until only his head was above the water. Holmes clove to the tree trunk, pressing her nipples, her pubic hair, through the ivy, onto the bark.

Moriarty's head went under.

The world had changed.

○

The next morning, as she usually did during the summer holidays, Watson came round.

'She's still in bed, lazy cow,' said Holmes' mum. 'You just go on up.'

Watson went in without knocking.

The curtains had been left undrawn and out the window Watson saw a tractor moving across the far end of the field.

'Are you awake?' Watson asked.

'Yes,' came a voice from under the covers.

'Did you see *Top of the Pops* last night?' asked Watson, sitting down at the end of the bed.

'No,' said Holmes.

'It was great,' said Watson, 'Morrissey was on.'

Holmes stuck a hand out and batted away the sheets. She looked into Watson's eyes.

'I saw him last night,'

'Who, Morrissey?' asked Watson.

'Moriarty.'

'Which band's he in?'

'Don't joke.'

'You mean you *really* saw him?'

'I saw him.'

'But we've been waiting all summer.'

'He was walking along through the field.'

'What, out there?'

'He walked to the pond and then he undressed – '

'He never.'

' – and he walked into the water.' Holmes reached up and tugged at one of the curtains.

'Did you see his cock?'

Holmes stood quickly up. She was still wearing the calico dress. 'I was standing behind The Kissing Tree.'

'Did you see it?'

'Don't ask such stupid questions, Watson,' Holmes stood where she had been standing last night, when.

'Sorry, Holmes,'

'There was a full moon. I saw him in the full moon.'

'So you followed him, did you?'

'Yes. I followed Moriarty.'

'Down to the pond – '

'I stood behind The Kissing Tree.'

'Did you speak to him?'

'Of course, I didn't,'

'What did he do when he came out of the water? Wasn't he soaking?'

Holmes went over to the wardrobe and started to go through her dresses. The hangers scraped lightly along the bar. Watson picked up the Mickey Mouse Alarm Clock. Mickey's little gloved white hands pointed to twelve and to three.

'What did he do, Holmes? Did he have a towel? He did get out, didn't he? You didn't just stand and watch him drown.'

Holmes spoke into the wardrobe: 'I'm not going to tell you, Watson. It's too dangerous. Moriarty is too dangerous.'

'But he's not dead, then, is he? He can't be dangerous if he's dead.'

'No, Watson,' said Holmes, turning round, 'Moriarty never dies. Not at the Reichenbach Falls, not ever.'

'That's a lovely dress, that,' said Watson.

'Watson. You must not tell a living soul of what I've seen. Not a living soul, you understand.'

'Yes, Holmes. Absolutely.'

'Would you wear this dress for me, Watson?'

○

The two girls walked out the front door, down the concrete-slab path and swung through the gate. The Hound of the Baskervilles yapped at them though next door's privet. They turned left, toward the village.

Holmes lived in the last house on the left: Number 8.

Watson was at Number 5.

The houses were all four-square semis, ludicrous in 1940s Council House pink. From a distance, on a blue sunny day, the windows and lintels looked sparkly white.

Number 6 had a satellite dish.

Altogether (before Moriarty's family moved in to Number 1) the four houses in the road contained eight households: seven women, three men, fourteen children.

Holmes was the only only child. Watson had a big brother. He worked on the farm. Most of the other children were toddlers. Even so, there wasn't much babysitting.

Holmes and Watson walked down the road, toward the village. As they passed Number 1, Holmes said:

'Keep looking straight ahead. He's in the garden. Don't look at him. Come on, run!'

They ran till they were hidden by the hedge.

Holmes walked along the smooth '70s tarmac, Watson on the scrotty thick-leaved grass of the verge.

'That was a close call, Holmes,' said Watson.

'We can't be too careful, Watson,' said Holmes.

'They must have moved in yesterday when we were in town.'

'Blast!'

'What is it, Holmes?'

'We could have seen so much about them, if only we'd been there. We could have seen what they meant.'

'How d'you think he knew about the pond? D'you think he was just exploring?'

'Moriarty always knows his way around. He is never lost. He sensed the pond. It called to him through the night.'

Up ahead they could see the church spire among its elms. A car went by, an Austin Allegro, small hands waving from the back window. Holmes and Watson waved back.

Holmes was the taller and prettier of the two: cream-pale skin, a precocious bob of black hair, dark green eyes. Only a slightly harsh profile threatened her present beauty, though it would later enhance it. Watson was a strawberry-blonde: plumpish, freckled.

'Was he really trying to kill himself, do you think?' asked Watson.

'How can one ever know how Moriarty thinks? He is the greatest criminal mind the world has ever known.'

'What does he look like?'

'It was dark.'

'But you said there was a moon – '

'He is tall, pale, with dark hair.'

'What – under his armpits and all?'

'Watson, you ask too many questions.'

'I'm sorry, Holmes, it's just I sort of have to, don't I. Or else you don't tell me anything.'

'You know all you need to know, Watson. Moriarty has moved into the road. We will never be safe again.'

'But do we want to be safe?' asked Watson.

Holmes only looked at her.

○

During the summer holidays, they visited the grave every morning.

Watson hadn't thought much of her father till he died, just before Easter. Only during the summer holidays did she realize how important he had been. It was nothing to do with love, more her sense of human scale. The house seemed like a mansion without him in it. She would get lost for days, walking down the stairs. Her mother was still sleeping on the settee. Her brother was now the man of the house, but her brother wasn't a man.

Holmes was a man. Holmes knew about grief. Holmes' father had left home when she was only two.

Holmes always said her father was a soldier, but she didn't really know. The only clue she had was a picture of him, his head sticking out of a Chieftain tank. He was wearing a beret with a badge on it, but he might have borrowed that.

Her mother never talked about him, and she'd only found the photograph by accident. It fell out of her mother's copy of *Lucky Jim*. Holmes kept it in her Evidence Box.

They walked through the churchyard and down to the lower field. The old graveyard was full. They'd had to start burying people close together, in tight rows.

Watson's father's grave was no different from all the others.

'Hello, Dad,' Watson said, before sitting down beside him.

'Hello, Watson's father,' said Holmes.

From the lower field, you could look down toward

the high brick walls of the farm. There was a rookery in the trees at the top of the next hill. The church bells rang for ten o'clock.

'Morrissey was great,' said Watson. 'I'm really sorry you missed him.'

'Watson, what would you do if you only had a few weeks to live?'

'How many?'

'Three or four.'

'I don't know. I'd like to go to London, to Baker Street. Just to see where we used to live.'

'Where I used to live.'

'Of course, Holmes.'

'Nothing else? Isn't there anything else you'd like to do?'

'It's not really worth it, is it? I haven't got any money to spend or give away. I don't really know anyone outside the road and the farm and the village.' She paused. 'Why, what would you do?'

'I didn't ask you so you'd ask me back.'

'But you must've thought about it to want to ask.'

'Not really. Only since last night. I think Moriarty is going to kill me.'

'Why?'

'Because Moriarty kills people. I feel doomed, just having seen him. I'm going to die.'

'Stop talking like that, Holmes. Especially here. It's bad luck, I'm sure.' Watson pulled a long hair out from the back of her head and blew it away off her palm. 'Go on!' she said to Holmes.

'It won't work,' said Holmes. 'I can't be protected.'

○

On the Market Square, they walked past the War Memorial kissing their thumbs and holding their breath.

In the shop, they bought two pints of milk each.

As they came out of the shop, they saw Number 4's Austin Allegro again. They put their cartons down and waved before picking them up and walking on.

About a hundred yards down the street, they stopped at a small house and rang the bell. Watson stood back, out of sight.

'Good morning, Gran,' said Holmes, when the door was open. 'Here's your milk.' She passed it through.

'Thank you, dear,' came a voice from the warm inside. 'Would you like some cake?'

'Not today, thank you, Gran, ' said Holmes. 'See you tomorrow,'

'Bye bye dear.'

○

They took the secret path back to Number 8, hoping that Moriarty hadn't discovered it yet.

Nettles stung their ankles and burrs stuck to their hems. The path went through inexplicable periods of heat and cold. Bees lunged heavily from one hedgerow to the other.

Just before it turned onto the road, the path ran along the far shore of the pond. Holmes and Watson stopped and sat down.

Holmes opened her milk carton, took several gulps and passed it to Watson.

'He was standing there,' she pointed.

Watson looked across at the foot-smooth earth.

'It must've been lovely.'

Holmes wiped her mouth with the back of her hand.

'Mum said we might be going into town this afternoon, d'you want to come?'

'No, Watson. I have to think about this. I have to think the whole thing through.'

Watson passed the carton back and Holmes finished it.

○

For the rest of the morning they sat in Holmes' room, talking. At about twelve, Watson went home for lunch.

She reappeared at the front door around one, her mum's Vauxhall buzzing in the road behind her.

'You sure you don't want to come?' she asked. 'We're going to have treats.'

Holmes waved over Watson's shoulder to Watson's mum.

'I'm sorry, Watson,' she said, 'this is more important than that. This is a matter of life and death.'

'Shouldn't I stay, then?' asked Watson, looking up the road.

'No. Go. You can't do anything here.'

○

When Watson got back early in the evening they went over to her house and sat in the living room, playing the Morrissey single over and over.

Watson sat in one of the armchairs while Holmes lay on the settee.

'He's magnificent,' said Watson.

'I don't think it's as good as his last one,' said Holmes.

'Maybe not,' said Watson, 'but he's still magnificent.'

O

That night, Moriarty again walked through the cornfield and down to the pond and, again, Holmes followed him, watching.

Exactly as before, Moriarty, leaving his clothes behind him, moved into and under the water.

The following morning, Holmes didn't get up when Watson came round.

Two mornings later, Holmes asked Watson not to disturb her before twelve.

A week later and Holmes changed that to two.

O

'Did you see him again last night?' Watson asked, sitting opposite Holmes at the kitchen table.

'Have you been taking the milk round to my gran's?' asked Holmes.

'Yes, I have.'

'Does she notice the difference? Does she know it's you and not me?'

'Of course she does.'

'I just wondered.' Holmes turned the spoon round in her cornflakes.

'Holmes, tell me what's happening.'

But Holmes' mum came in with the shopping and they had to talk about *Brookside*.

○

'I'm getting worried about you,' said Holmes' mum, when Watson had finally gone. 'It's not good, this lying in bed all the time. Get out and do something with your time.'

'Mum,' said Holmes.

'It'll be a good thing for you when school starts back up again.'

'Mum,'

'I don't know how you can stand it, up in that little room all the time, with all this lovely country to go into outdoors – and we've had such beautiful weather.'

Holmes stood up.

'Aren't you going to watch *Coronation Street* either?'

'Not tonight, Mum.'

'It's not – you know – "our friend" – is it?'

'Everything's not that, Mum.'

Holmes moved towards the stairs.

'And I want to wash that dress as well.'

○

At the end of another week of watchings, Holmes went to see her gran.

'Well, we haven't seen you for a while, have we?' said Gran. 'I was just putting a bit of Brasso over these here. They'll be yours, one day, when you're grown up. They were my mother's once.'

'Gran, if I tell you something, you won't tell Mum, will you?'

'Now, I can't make promises like that on nothing, love. If it's something awful, like a little baby, I'd have to tell her. It wouldn't feel right, not. You understand that. She'd have a right to know.'

'It's not awful. Well, it is. But it's not really, not like what you mean.'

'Let's sit down and get comfy then and then you can tell it.'

They moved through into the living room and sat down on the Velux armchairs on either side of the gas. Holmes looked up at her grandfather's collection of toby jugs. Gran's eyes followed hers.

'Silly old fool *he* was,' she said. 'He thought they'd be worth a fortune, one day. Like on the telly.'

'Perhaps they are,' said Holmes.

'I suppose so,' said Gran. 'Now what is it, love?'

Holmes felt the doily tickling the back of her neck.

'I'm sorry, Gran, it's nothing. I shouldn't've said.'

'How about some tea? We can talk after.'

But, when the tea came, Holmes got Gran onto the harvest and then the war.

○

Holmes spent the next three nights trying to sleep, trying not to follow Moriarty. That she failed in her resolution, going every time, finally decided Holmes on the correct course of action. Things had been turning very bad, recently. Watson had stopped coming round. School was only three decades away. Her mother thought she was on drugs.

○

On the morning of the chosen day, Holmes wrote her will. In it she left everything to Watson.

With the money in her savings account, Watson was to go to London and buy a record player.

Special instructions were left about the location and disposal of the Evidence Box.

Holmes wrote special messages to her mum and her gran.

In the afternoon, Holmes went with Watson to the grave. Watson started crying almost immediately.

'What is it, Watson?'

'Nothing, Holmes.'

'I have treated you abominably.'

'I don't want him dead. I did, you know, when he was alive. I even prayed sometimes for it. And when it happened, I was really pleased for a while. I was pleased at the funeral, because I thought he was sort of pretending and would come back a different person. But, then, now, I feel like it was me that killed him by hating him. If I hadn't've wanted it, it wouldn't've happened. Oh Holmes, I'm so horrible.'

Holmes hugged Watson.

'Now listen to me, Watson — you are not to blame in this matter. I believe you are innocent of the murder of your father. His case is, indeed, a great mystery, but we shall solve it one day. Thinking that you are guilty isn't going to help. It doesn't help him and it doesn't help you.'

'But you didn't even have a father! I feel so greedy that I did.'

'Tell me, Watson, why have you never spied on Moriarty?'

Watson sat up and blew her nose into a tissue.

'Because you warned me he was the most dangerous criminal in the world.'

'So you never even stayed awake to see what he looked like?'

'I drew the curtains before it even got dark.'

'Oh, Watson,' said Holmes, sniffing, 'was there ever a truer more loyal friend than you?'

'I'd be very sorry if there wasn't,' said Watson. 'I'm such a wet and a weed.'

They laughed at each other for a while.

'Tonight — can you meet me tonight, at three o'clock, round on the secret path side of the pond?'

'Of course, Holmes.'

'Dress in warm dark clothes and don't bring a torch or anything. There will be a moon. The last one, I think, probably. The last moon of the summer. Tomorrow they cut down the corn and kill all the animals. Tomorrow is the real end of things.'

○

When she got home, Holmes tore the will up and flushed it down the loo.

She watched *Coronation Street* and *Brookside* with her mother.

○

Holmes had been right. The moon, though partial, gave enough of the edges of things.

Watson shivered with the excitement of sneaking out of the house and then with the chill of the air.

Number 1 had a light on, downstairs.

The graveyard as she passed it was full of believable ghosts.

Stumbling down the secret path, spiderstrands tickled up her nose.

When she got to the pond, Holmes was there waiting.

'He hasn't been, has he?'

'Three o'clock – every night.'

'What's the time now?'

'Two fifteen.'

'I've never done this before, Holmes. Sneaking out, I mean.'

Holmes was looking in the direction Moriarty would come from.

Through the branches of The Kissing Tree, against the glow of the town, she could see the TV aerial of her house.

'I hate it when they cut the corn and you can hear the mice squealing.'

'Can you really, Watson?'

'I don't know. Perhaps they never really stop. If you listen closely enough, they're always there. Even in winter, when they're really not. Holmes what are we going to do? Are you going to tell me?'

'Yes, Watson, I am. You are my best friend of all, Watson. I have been very mean to you over the last few decades. I haven't let you in at all. There are more important things than just – '

'Than what, Holmes?'

'You are very important to me, Watson. But now I must tell you what we are going to do.'

○

Moriarty came through the cornfield, as he always did, just before three o'clock.

The moonlight was fluttering out.

He walked a little faster than usual. It was colder and the water would be colder still.

An upstairs light was on in the house at the end. Usually, all the lights in the road were out, except for the TV in Number 6.

Moriarty stopped for a glance up at the window. A tall figure moved across and back, once, twice.

As he moved toward the pond, Moriarty rode his hands, palms down, over the surface of the corn.

He felt the ripe heads knocking against the knuckles of his thumbs and the bristles flicking between his fingers.

He began his ritual song: Father–Mother–Father–Mother–Father–Mother.

The ground swung down to the poolside.

He positioned himself correctly and began the undressing. Jumper. Shoes. Trousers.

The coldness of the air was a new kind of difference.

He moved toward the water less openly than before.

He wanted to cup his palms over his nipples, but knew that wasn't allowed.

The water round his ankles was molten.

He sang louder and slowly forced himself on, in, under, again.

He opened his eyes, though there was nothing to see except the chance of moonlight. His eyes would sting tomorrow, but that was part of the honesty. Like the clothes. Like the cold.

He let his legs float up behind him. He looked down into the water. His buttocks were now the only part of him on the surface. He felt them pimpling against the air.

For as long as he could, he held. Then five counts more. Then another five. Then five. Then another. Then ten.

When he burst up out of the water, he saw immediately that something had altered.

The usual composition – of pond, trees, sky, moon, clouds – had been disturbed.

There was an extra square of whiteness.

He looked toward it.

Standing by the pond on the opposite side were two naked women, looking at him, holding hands.

# Mr Kipling

Mr Kipling, as you no doubt already know, makes *exceedingly* good cakes; and has done now for about as long as most of us can remember, though it was, in fact, only 1967 that he first came to public notice. What I would not expect you to know is that Mr Kipling is the best friend I have in the world. We correspond. I write to him, almost daily now, telling him of the small travails of my small life, and he replies, under a pseudonym, politely denying that he exists. He is so kind. He claims that he is merely the invention of an advertising executive, established in order to humanize a rather soggy line of cakes and biscuits. He only admitted this after a very long while; before then, he thanked me for my letters, and was afraid that he couldn't help, but was glad that I enjoyed his products. He sometimes even sent me a token. I have them, framed, up above my desk. It is a 'quiet country retreat' I have here. In fact, there is an orchard out back not dissimilar to the one in which the apples for Mr Kipling's Bramley Apple Pies are picked. There is a village postmistress, who is the 'bane' of my life. She looks like a rabid wolf and, I am sure, steams open my letters. Her name is Miss Blood. My neighbours, on the left side, dress their children in Christmas jumpers and, during the summer, walk around in rather less than was considered proper in Mr Kipling's day; on the right side, I have the dairy farm: Mrs Jones is constantly threatening but never delivering children. I live alone and am trying to get some money from the National Trust to repair the roof. It is thatched, but has not been redone since the Jubilee, when a rather shoddy job was made of it. Thatched roofs have never done particularly well under Labour governments. At four o'clock every afternoon, just as Noël Coward would have it, everything 'stops' for tea. Mr Kipling is with me in spirit. I always pour him a cup and put a little treat on his plate. Some people would say that surely by now Mr Kipling must be rather tired of eating his own cakes, but I believe that – given the prestigious circumstances (the oaken walls, the cheery log fire, the sympathetic company) – Mr Kipling could always be prevailed upon to partake. If not, then he is a different man from the one I take him for. Yesterday, it was his Battenberg Treats that I did justice to; today, Saturday, the Glazed Fruit Tartlets; tomorrow, I have not yet decided. Perhaps the Lemon Slices or perhaps the Almond. They know me of 'old' in the Village Shop, and tell me whenever Mr Kipling is preparing an innovation. 'Oh, he's harmless enough,' I heard Mrs Poon say, as I left the other day. I wonder how anyone could ever think Mr Kipling capable of harm? There was a new girl. Miss Ogbuku. I think she may diminish the pleasures of shopping. Mrs Poon anticipates me in everything, and I hope she is not thinking of retiring. Mrs Poon is only middle-aged. She does not attend church. Mr Kipling does. Mr Kipling is a High Anglican, like myself. I suspect, though, that he has more of an inclination toward Rome than I do. The occasional overuse of cinnamon in his Mince Pies tells me so. Who cannot be sensible of the lure of further incense and plusher robes? A more august tradition and a bloodier roll of honour? But I will not desert the church of Betjeman and Larkin. And Mr Kipling will never, I trust, go to Rome. I have in my letters warned him off Jesuitical dinner parties and other Popish dabblings. I believe I have made him fully aware of their dangerous allure. Such a distinguished convert, no doubt, has great attractions for them. In a way, if Mr Kipling were suborned, it would undermine the constitutional position of the Church of England. I don't quite know how, but it would. Mr Kipling does not take Earl Grey tea, being more desirous of robuster flavours; and to take, as he does, 'Three sugars, please,' in that Queen of Teas would inevitably lead to suspicions of effeminacy and, indeed, of Sodomism. No, Mr Kipling has his three heaped teaspoons in a small china cup of fine but strong Assam. I can't stand the stuff myself. We pipe smokers have a phrase for what happens when the accumulated tobacco finds its noxious way into the mouth, we call it Arab's Armpit: that is how Assam tastes to me. Mr Kipling does not smoke a pipe; he likes a long cool cigar, and I always make sure to have some in. Mr Kipling is a widower, totally devoted to his culinary craft. Mrs Kipling, sadly, died a number of years ago. They met during the blitz, when she was the prettiest girl in the shelter, and he the dashingest man. They were happily married for 30 years. She supported him through his early struggles. She never cooked. It was a great grief to him when she passed away. He went through one of his darker periods. I like to think that the Rich Chocolate Tart is his posthumous tribute to a passion whose strength he hardly realized until it was too late. There is certainly something mournful and even gothic about this creation. A 'requiem' in chocolate. Mrs Kipling is with the angels now, looking down upon Mr Kipling and blessing him and his work. I often pray to Mrs Kipling to intercede for me when, as it does, temptation overtakes me. The Own Brand Devils dance before my eyes and the Discount Demons whisper. Of course Mr Kipling's cakes are more expensive; it is because they contain love and compassion and, even, grief. I believe Mr Kipling would be the ideal man to provide flavoured wafers for the Mass, if such a measure were ever introduced to encourage new worshippers into our churches. His every recipe is a homily, his every baking, a prayer. That he makes Angel Cakes is hardly surprising. It is a great joy to him that his many nephews come to visit him at Christmas. He sometimes can be prevailed upon to put on his Santa Claus costume. The Mince Pies which he proffers during the festive season are his own humble offering to the Lamb of God. How integral they are to so many people's celebrations! On Christmas Eve, I always raise a glass of sherry to Mr Kipling, for his sterling efforts yet again in providing the larger part of the nation with their Yuletide fare. It is an heroic yet humble achievement, recalling his experiences during the Blitz. I believe we may even have fire-watched together, once or twice.

# Z-ward, BoJo, Kenneth
# and the BetamaxBoy

>mail
to: edward.z@demon.co.uk
from: bojo@easynet.co.uk
subj: some pretty weirdshit

<):-(> zed, my old e-mate. FYUA: this shit. another
e-friend brwsd it s/w on the net. MF wont gimme the
siteinfo, so maybe hes untruthing me. (homepage s/w,
I guess) jst got no netiquette, some gs. flame the fuck,
zwot I say. anyways, my co-con o/t wd&wnrfl, thought ya
might dig. BTW, its some PFHeavyS. dont let it f with
your m, bigbuddy. mail/fax me back when brwsd. quick-
time. BoJo.

○

Hi. My netname is BetamaxBoy – which explains a lot of
what follows. To keep things simple, let me explain: I call
myself BetamaxBoy because I collect Betamax videos
(tapes and players) from the late '70s and early '80s.
As you all know, these beautiful artefacts aren't exactly
available in Tandy nowadays, so I have to go hunting for
them in junkshops and at carbootsales. I own about 64
by now – 57 of them work, 5 I'm cannibalizing and 2

I'm repairing. (My room's just full of this shit!) Why'd I like them, you ask? I just like that particular tone of fuzz they come up with, round the edges especially. VHS just never did it for me in the same way – that's why I'm the BetamaxBoy. I can't explain – you either love it or you don't. Some guys go for Pamela Anderson and some for Winona Ryder (Myself, I'm a Winona-kinda-guy) – who knows why? I just love this shit. It's such a shame that Betamax lost out to VHS. (Boo! Hiss!) It was such a superiorsystem. But then, if Betamax wasn't a cult-type-thing, I wouldn't have gotten into it. Or I'd be the VHS-Vampire, instead. (Okay, so I'm a sad fucker with no friends. Sosumi.) Winona's not exactly a cult, I know. Not after _Dracula_. But anyway. Don't get me started. Well, about a month ago, I suppose, I was at this carbootsale in Devon (I was in the area; really, I was) and I wasn't having any luck with the players, but there was this one bloke who had a cardboardboxful of tapes – like 20 or 30 – which of course I bought straight off. £10 the lot, though I coulda had em for £5. He was glad to get shot of them. He said he'd been going to dump them. He'd been bringing them along for weeks. He was giving them one last chance. My babies! *One last chance.* 'They're not even mine,' he said 'I'm just doing it for a mate. Take my advice, mate. *Never* agree to do things for mates.' You can imagine how impatient I was to slot them in and hear them go kerchunk-whirr and watch the pictures fuzz on up. Adjust the tracking. Kick back, relax, enjoy. But I didn't get home till the following evening. (I'm a day's drive from Devon, thrill-seekers: figure that out.) I got home, got a pizza delivered (pepperoni with extra anchovies, pineapple, onions and corn: this was a special occasion), chowed down, hit the fastforwardbutton. Mostly it was old episodes of _Crossroads_ and _Coronation Street_. Worth watching for the ads, which were hilarious, and the haircuts, which were even funnier. (The haircuts *in* the ads almost crippled me.) Then there were a couple of movies: _The Cannonball Run_, _The Bitch_, _Escape from Alcatraz_. Even something as up to date as _Top Gun_ (1989). Videoed off SkyTV. That gave me a bit of a boner, I have to admit: to think some lovely schmuck paid all that money for a sattelitedish, but still stuck with his faithful old Betamax video. So touching. I love people like that. People like me. Best of all were two episodes of _Champion, The Wonder Horse_ and one of the original _Buck Rogers_ (none of this 21st Century shit: I'm a Rogers purist – I want to be able to *see* the wires holding the rockets up; I want the rockets to goddam wobble *just* before they land!). Then there was this one tape, nothing written on it, no box, no label. I came to it almost last. (You know how you save these things up.) Chunked it in. It was nothing from the TV. Just this guy, pretty nerdy looking, sitting in this weird room – lavalamps and Hendrixposters – 60stimewarp – talking direct to camera – B/W UK 1994-5 23mins. And I just couldn't believe that, on top of all the rest, there was someone out there who *still* had a camera that could tape onto Betamax. This is, like, ten years at least after the fact. It touched me to my very soul, let me tell you, ladiesngentlemen. I almost cried. It was an Elvismoment. I loved him tender. And I could tell he'd done this tape only quite recently because of all the shit he was mentioning (you'll see) – tvshows and camcorders. Modern stuff. He was a funnylooking guy: Lennonspecs (1966), Maccalips (1968), Ringonose (1970), Georgehair (1972). Your commonorgarden park-bench beardyweirdy. What he was saying made a lot of sense to me. I watched it through a couple of times that night, then 5 the following day. (Heck, it was a Sunday.) By the end of the day, I'd decided I had to somehow get this shit out to the people. So, I taped it onto audio, sat down and transcribed it, word for word, onto the Mac. Then I watched the tape through a few more times, and wrote a few descriptions of what the guy (I call him Kenneth, like in the REMsong) looks like and what he's doing. Anyway, enough. It took me a few weeks, like I say, to get right. But here it is, folks: Kenneth's Words of Wisdom as Faithfully Transcribed by the BetamaxBoy:

Hi ... um ... I haven't really, um [I figured I'd leave in the ums, for, like, atmosphere], prepared anything *specific*, though I've got a few specific ideas I'd like to get across, record for posterity ... There's a few things [Holds up, with some difficulty, copy of _The Columbia Enyclopedia_, 5th Edition, 1994] that I've got handy to, like, quote from [I, like, like likes like Kenneth's likes], but this is all off of the top of my head – so if it's a bit of a riff, a bit fragmentary, then ... um ... that's what it is. Okay? Now, listen up. I want you to, like, follow me for a while – I am not a weirdopsycholoonie. Whatever people may have said or written about me, I am not a weirdo. And I am not paranoid, however hard the forces try to make me. [That could be The Forces, if you want it.] Now, I've got a concept for you, just to loosen you up: Everything you've ever heard is true and you mustn't believe anything you read in the papers. Alright? The earth is flat because Lee Harvey Oswald did *not* shoot Jack Ruby. Got that? And, thirdly (and most importantly): It's all a plot. I repeat: It is all a plot. It all connects. There are, like, subterranean passages between things that you and I are only vaguely aware of. [Takes off glasses and begins to clean them. Kenneth has beautiful big brown eyes.] Excuse me ... um ... Now, this may sound a bit overboard, but, like, I think I've worked out a way to map these passages. So what I'm giving you here is, like, the dope, okay? ... the inside track ... the real heavy shit, kapish? Remember: Everything you've heard is true and don't believe anything you read. Ever. It's like a kind of Buddhist thing. [Puts glasses back on, having finished cleaning them.] That's how you understand it: by not understanding it. By saying shit to understanding. But, like, what I've got to say to you today is, like, this: I've traced the map, I've, like, followed the passages, I've seen where they lead: they lead to one person, one single man, the importance of whom it is impossible to overestimate. [Kenneth picks up scrappy oblongpiece of brownpaper. It's a Giroenvelope. Kenneth reads it a little, then chucks it over his shoulder.] Got that right, anyway. And who is this man, I hear you ask? Tell us! Tell us! [Kenneth starts to get really hyped around this point. Like he was making a speech, or something.] Well, wait a little longer, friends, I want to explain why he's so important. Do you know what, like, the effect of a paradigm is? It's like a model for something – like what you press jelly out of. It makes stuff into, like, stuff with shape. It can even happen with numbers. EequalsMCsquared. That's like a paradigm. Do you get it? If not, stop and get a dictionary. Freezeframe me, and fucking look it up. Paradigm. P. A. R. A. D. I. G. M. Well, this man is the ultimate *paradigm* of modern British Society. He is the template from which the NewMan will be pressed. And what I want to tell you is, he's dangerous. Don't let him affect you. What he stands for is evil. Evil. His name – God, it almost rhymes with it – is Beadle. Jeremy Beadle. Stop it. [Kenneth gets very agitated.] Stop it! I know some of you are laughing now. Laughing at me. Don't. Or I'll – [Kenneth picks up gun from between his legs, presses it to his right temple, pulls the trigger. A little flag with BANG on it unfunnily slaps his forehead.] I will. I fucking will. If Kurt can do it, I can do it. Brains all over the fucking wall, man. So, like, believe me, or else. Or just give me a chance to explain it all. Please. [Kenneth goes down on his knees. Holds up hands as if to pray or plead.] Wait a moment ... um ... where the fuck am I ... Jeremy Beadle! [Holds up poster of Jeremy Beadle. Fuck knows where he got it. There is a scribble in the bottom righthand corner which may or may not be a signature.] Who is this man? First, I assume you know who he is. You've seen his shows. Or at least know their concepts. So, I assume you know him. I assume you know what a shitload of gunk he's made out of. Look at him! Look at him! [Thrusts poster at camera. There Beadle stands, greysuited, scuzzbearded: the glintyeyed, grinning, bastard son of a whore, a hamster and a dentaltechnician.] He is actually deformed. [I think

Kenneth goes a little too far here.] You can't see it in this photo, because of course he's hiding it, but he has, like, a little iddybiddy righthand. It's, like, his trademark. People watch his shows, like, partly in order to see it. It's a fucking freakshow. Most of the time, he hides it, like, behind his back, or, like, puts it down by his side, or in his pocket – places where it looks like a normalhand. But sometimes he gets brave and, like, waves it around. [Kenneth gesticulates wildly, like a robot wanking off a giraffe.] Once, I even saw him stroke the head of a child with it! Shit ! But, like I said, most of the time he just swings it around, using it as the baton to conduct his show, to mark out the rhythms of his hypnoticspeech. Jeremy Beadle. Let us examine this man's career as closely as we can. What is the principle upon which this specimen's entire televisual existence had been based? Friends, I'll tell you – surveillance. From the very start. From the moment _Game For A Laugh_ first aired, in 1981. Who can ever forget the catchphrase with which the show that made him famous used to end: _And don't forget,_ the four of them used to say, those grinning gits, _we'll be watching you watching us watching you watching us – at the same time next week. So, tune in then._ What followed? What followed this? _You've Been Framed_. Another show in which Beadle spied upon people – in which Beadle made a joke out of it. And then came _Beadle's About_. _Beadle's About_ with, of course, the implied jingle _Look out! Look out! Beadle's about!_ For that's what it is: our own naturalizedversion of _Candid Camera_. And what was that other one called? The one in-between. Something – shit!

I've forgotten. I had a list somewhere. [Looks on floor.]
But do you notice, friends, in each case the movement,
the tendency, away from 'staged' funnies toward
'spontaneous' ones [I put these in quotes, as I think
Kenneth would have wanted me to. Something in his
manner suggests it, though he avoids using airscallops.]
– away from professionalcamerawork toward amateur-
camcording. *Watching You Watching Us* has become
*Watching Us Watching Us*. Money is offered for our
clips, our funnies. Well this is my funny, Beadle-ma-boy.
Like it! Like it? [Kenneth, I'm afraid to say, moons the
camera. Written on his bumcheeks are the words _Like_
and _It?_] We watch ourselves hurting ourselves,
disgracing ourselves. [Just like you did then, Ken.]
Beadle watches with us. I won't mention now how we,
the human race, are, like, being systematically
cartoonized. I mean, it'd be wonderful: if only our teeth
*did* regrow between scenes, like Tom's; if only we
*were* as bullet/baseballbat/bombproof as Jerry. But
we're not. We're squashy, full of bones, and when you
splat us we stay splatted. Now, what are we faced with
here but a normalization of surveillance? It's only a bit of
fun. It's only a laugh. But etymology. E. Fucking.
T. Y. M. O. Fucking. L. O. G. Fucking. Y. Etymology
doesn't lie. Etymology shows us. The definition of Beadle
in the dictionary is – Wait a minute. [Kenneth hunts
for dictionary, finds it, turns pages until – ] Beadle:


ceremonial officer of church, college, city,
company, etc.; (Hist.) – that's historicalmeaning –

parish officer nah nah appointed by vestry – shit,
better look that up as well – vestry to keep order
in church – you see, you see! – etc., (Sc.) –
that's Scottish, though it should be scumbag or
scuzzface – church official officer attending on
the minister – yo! Beadle, attend to me! – hence
Beadledom – listen up – stupid officiousness –
stupid – officiousness – and the next word is
beady, like in 'beadyeyes' and the next word is
'beagle' as in trackerdogs and the next is 'beak'
like in oldblackandwhitefilms, the headmaster –
then 'beam' like xrays and shit – then 'beast' –
and that's etymology

[Kenneth slams shut the dictionary.] Is this an accident?
I ask you! Here is the televisualpoliceman. The man
to keep us in order. The ThoughtPolice. This man is
the face on our telescreens. He is tempting us into a
state of total selfsurveillance. Why miss these hilarious-
moments? Why miss out on the chance of £200? Why
not camcord everything all the time? The more tapes,
the more bloopers! It's coming, believe me, it's coming.
The entry in _The Columbia Encyclopedia_, under
_Photography_ which I looked up a few days ago, says
this: [Bends down to read from _Encyclopedia_, which
is obviously laid out on the floor.]

The inception of these visualdocuments of
personal and public history engendered vast
changes in people's perception of history, of time
and of themselves. The concept of privacy – listen,
people – was greatly altered as cameras were used

to record most areas of human life. The ubiquitous presence of photographic machinery eventually changed humankind's sense of what was suitable for observation.

That's some heavyshit. _Changed humankind's sense of what was suitable_. And the camcorder? Because photographs are so easilystaged. A smile: hold it for an instant and it's fixed for eternity. You could've been scowling the moment before; you can go back to scowling the moment after, but the smile is forever. [Kenneth smiles. Badteeth, man.] Freezeframe me now. [Kenneth smiles for thirtysevenseconds.] But the camcorder, the camcorder – its natural motion is forwards. Backwards almost never: backwards leads to potholes, lowhangingbranches, cliffs. It isn't safe to walk backwards with a camcorder. The camcorder is an investigativedevice. If the cat has darted behind the settee to hide, the camcorder will follow – it will follow because it can. [Kenneth mimes holding a camcorder. Thrusting it forwards. He thrusts a bit hard and hits the camera, which falls over. We have about half a minute of shots of the ceiling, the paperglobe lanternlightshade, Kenneth'snostrils. Perhaps I should say here and now that I don't absolutely agree with everything Kenneth says, just parts, here and there. But you have to admit, the guy is way cool.] The camcorder's investigation is perpetual and, while it's going on, uninterrupted. It is very difficult to stage a camcording: people aren't rehearsed enough, they forget themselves and so reveal themselves; they try to be themselves, and fail, and so

again display their realselves. Life only happens once.
The camcorder is there, all the time. It pursues, remains
unedited, uneditable. All life lived in its gaze is lived for
futurerepetition, for future erasure. Life happens as
many times as you want it to. Your grandfather can
dive into the swimmingpool, from the highboard, until
eternity – but he cannot love his wife. He cannot do
anything he didn't. Because he was only filmed.
You can now – you can decide to camcord everything.
Your life can be a videojukebox. Fuck your wife, on
video. You can fuck her again, after she's dead. On
video. Your grandfather couldn't do that. Your grandfather fought in the firstworldwar and killed Germans.
He lost his penis on the Westernfront. Your grandfather
ran twelve miles with his penis in his hand. And a nurse
sewed it back on. And he married that nurse. Yes!
And she was your grandmother. And she was the only
woman that ever knew how to handle your grandfather's
penis, because she'd sewed it on upside down. And
I'm losing it, aren't I? That's not what I'm arguing about.
Penises and the firstworldwar and shit. It's probably this
camera here now, recording me. I'm speaking to camera
now. The camera doesn't like what I'm saying. It is
aggressing me, trying to put me off. [Kenneth spits at
camera, misses.] I need a break. I'm going to the
bathroom – I mean the toilet – I'll be back in a minute –
I'll just leave it running – Please fastforward – [Kenneth
moves offcamera.] If you don't want to, I'll put a little
music on – Hang on. There you are: REM's _Murmur_,
_A Perfect Circle_. [Kenneth (you see why I call him that
now) disappears for about 2:37. We hear a couple of

doors openandshut, openandshut. The distant flush of a toilet. Doors. Kenneth is back.] I like REM. I hope you do too. Anyway, where were we? Ah, I remember: I'd just completely lost the thread. But my subject remains the same: Jeremy Beadle. *Now* do you see what I mean by paradigm? Beadle is encouraging us to become accustomed to our surveillance – so that when we go out shopping in our local ShoppingCentre on Saturdayafternoon, the fact that we are videoed almost every step of the way doesn't bother us as much as it might. So that when a securitycamera appears, to tape us as we sit on the top deck of a bus, we don't think of it as at all unusual. So that when we hear there's hardly a sidestreet in the whole of Newcastletowncentre that isn't taped 24hours a day, we're quite chuffed at being so important. So when 2 young boys in Liverpool abduct another little boy, for the purpose of stoving his skull in, we can watch them as they do it – watch them and feel sortof cosy that they were spotted, that the videoimage helped solve the crime. Noone said that the videoimage *was* the crime. Noone said – STOP! I don't want to be taped! Turn those cameras off! Rip them down! Smash their lenses! Stamp on their MemorexCassettes! And why not? Why not? Because _Beadle's About_. That's why the man's a paradigm! – That's why the man is evil! – That's why the man must be killed! [Kenneth rips up poster of Beadle. Does various other things with it, that I don't want to describe. Eventually steps forward, behind the camera. The tape ends here.]

BB again. Now you'll understand that I don't want
anyone going and killing anyone. I thought I might
cut that last bit out, but decided you were all sensible
people. Kenneth, if you're out there, man: just chill,
okay? Don't fuck with your head so much. To the rest
of yous, if you enjoyed this and are interested in seeing
the tape (or if you have some Betamaxvideos to sell)
email me on: b.boy@demon.co.uk

○

> mail

to: alt.culture
from: edward.z.@demon.co.uk
subject: HOLY holy HOLY

Today, The REVELATION Came! Oh Great DAY of
DISCOVERY. Long TIME Coming. Praise BE. And The
REVELATION Came In the FORM Of an EMAIL. From
BoJo, The Putz, Of ALL People. STUPID BoJo. BoJo
who I NEVER REALLY LIKED. BoJo Who KNOWS Too
Much. BetamaxBoy, KENNETH'S False Prophet Tells Us
NOT To KILL The Beadle. THE Beadle Exists In ALL of
US. We Must FIGHT The Beadle Within, In The NAME of
KENNETH. We MUST Be Vigilant and INVISIBLE.
For BY His CASSETTE, Revealed Only To His FALSE
Prophet, the BetamaxBoy, KENNETH Has Delivered His
TOTAL MESSAGE. Yesterday, and LAST Week, AND
The WHOLE of Last MONTH, I DID Not Know. But Now,
NOW I RENOUNCE My Former SELF. I, Z-ward, Pledge

MYSELF to the Eternal STRUGGLE, in KENNETH'S
Name, Against The Beadle AND All his WORKS. I,
Z-ward, Have SCANNED This HOLY Holy Holy Text,
From Start TO Finish, So YOU, CHILDREN of the Net,
MAY Judge: WHO, Children, is KENNETH'S True
PROPHET? The MOCKERS, the Judas BROTHERS,
BoJo and BetamaxBoy, or I, Z-ward? This PAGE I Type
Up Is His Testament. For I, Z-ward, AM KENNETH'S
True PROPHET. I Command YOU, My CHILDREN, to
Use THE Weapons of INVISIBILITY. For Through the
NET, We ARE Invisible; On The Net, We May CHOOSE
To be WHOM We Desire. They CHOSE To Be BoJo
AND BetamaxBoy. THEY are The False PROPHETS.
They Must DIE. I AM Z-WARD. I AM ZED. NEITHER
Male NOR Female – Merely email. KENNETH Was
Given To US as A SIGN. KENNETH has APPEARED.
And THROUGH The Suicide of His Appearance,
ON the OCCASION of his TAPING, KENNETH Made a
Sacrifice TO Us Of His OWN Image. This Image WAS
Delivered To THE BetamaxBoy. The BetamaxBoy
ALONE Has Seen His FACE. THE BETAMAXBOY is
THE First False Prophet. FOR this Reason, The
BetamaxBoy MUST Die. FIND The BetamaxBoy,
CHILDREN of KENNETH! Find HIM, My Children!
KILL HIM! KILL BETAMAXBOY! But LEAVE BoJo and
The Beadle to ME. Z-ward.

Attach document:

# HMV

All the bright long English morning, quite without
knowing it, I have been different from, and I must even
despite the fear of the unjustifiable accusation of vanitas
say lesser than, myself – from myself, that is, as deliberately intended. Of course, subsequently, with the 'dark
backward and abysm' of embarrassment and execration
all before one, the thing becomes all the more awful for
its obvious obviousness. How I could not have known –
how, indeed, I could have forgotten – finally, how I was
so basely stupid as not to realize, not, as the phrases have
it, to 'twig', to 'grasp', to 'savvy'; these are things I do
not know. Perhaps it is the acknowledged eternal
discredit of my self-inflicted ignorance that I am, by
this small note to myself – and, please God, to no soul
else – attempting belatedly, unhopefully, pathetically to
balance out. Yes, *mon ange*, before you I am mortifying
myself; in your presence, I kneel; on your mercy and
care all my dignity retains.

So, to the obvious thing of which I knew nothing –
I now see that I all morning had positively been assailed
by anonymous and all too personable kindnesses.
Everyone, it seems, was 'in' on the joke – everyone
except myself, the joke. I was in a state of what was
something more than ignorance – for that would imply

the specific fact, the fact of which I knew nothing, but this was a more profound lack than just that; this was ignorance of ignorance, ignorance of the fact of facts. My mind was elsewhere, upon other non-quotidian business; and the objects with which it was concerned were those of affection and ingratiation, rather than appearance and, sad to say, reality. And so, ethereal and amorous as I was, though the supreme object was at that moment an ethereality again of my own creation – a certain Kate Croy of whom you shall know more, later – I did not, could not, recommend myself to the signs which were populating my vision, if not my sight. Men were mirrors to me, women also; all I saw was the labour of my own fashioning. The hints, therefore, the gestures, nods, inclinations, eye-dips, the meaning coughs and hums, the whole human repertoire of public information and social alert – all was as lost upon me as I was lost to it all.

The shop assistants, to their credit, were among the more subtle in their approach – though their discretion, in the end, was the downfall of their endeavour. What I for once wanted was that which I all but obsessively steadfastly avoid: the crass. Even, I suppose I must in all honesty add, the downright insulting would, upon this singular (this I think should be stressed) occasion, have been if not immediately welcome then at least subsequently appreciated. Perhaps it is an indication of the quality of the public servants in the employ of my most frequented London amenities, though no testament to their social daring – which perhaps is good – that such in the end futile subtleties were the means they employed to bring me to a greater consciousness of my unwonted disclosure.

Friends, of whom I met a number, were even more superfine in their communications – and so similarly unsuccessful. What is most interesting, from the hidden retrospect of Lamb House, is that they for the most part attempted to employ the verbal rather than the physical glance. The number of puns which I missed and which now, at this very moment, assail me like shafts of belated goodwill, is indeed legion. I feel, to coin an image, rather like a man must feel who, safely having swum the distance to shore from the vessel of his calamity, is there greeted by a large crowd who proceed to hurl ropes and buoyancy rings and empty barrels and advice of varying and conflicting sorts at him. What previously might have helped now only harms. That the lacerations are internal and retrospective makes them in no way less gushing, less gruesome. New barbs of innuendo fix themselves upon me instantly, and blood is drawn – chiefly to the cheeks and to the forehead. Oh God, even such an oaf as *he* – in all the smugness of gaudy tweed and the ingratiation of an overwaxed moustache – even C. P-S. made oblique mention. (As I remember, would I did not, he batted an imaginary blue-bottle – and remarked upon their proliferation during the summer months. 'Must,' he said, 'be something to do with the wind.' My perplexion then must equal my mortification now – for I had observed no such phenomenon, and took little trouble in telling him so.) He left me on Bond Street, at the corner, unceremoniously. I see now his reasons, but that does not I'm afraid ingratiate him to me – nothing, I think, would, unless it were perhaps cabled news of his immediate emigration for Australasia or Nova Scotia as attempted cure for a total prostration and insuperable dumbness, dating from the very instant he left my sight. (But though *he* may, Bond Street and Regent Street and Oxford Street in their totality will not.) More likely, he is 'dining out' this very evening upon the anecdote – though surely the Music Hall would even be above such vulgarity, even implicit. Society, though, is transcendently tolerant (of innuendo) and infinitely credulous (of slander). I cannot therefore be disappointed in him if this mode of self-nourishment and self-aggrandizement is what he chooses, the fault is really all my own – such an imbecile has few enough opportunities for wit; offer him the merest glim, and he will reach – offer him tangibility, he seizes. The real deep blame cannot rest upon any but myself, for it was myself that made the forgetfulness, created the unsafe condition, allowed all the various required absences. I admit I had last night given my butler, Greaves, leave to remain here in Lamb House – to which I this afternoon fled – in attendance of his wife, Betty, before coming away to my Hotel yestereve. In the morning, preparatory for lunching in the usual place with the usual friend, I dressed myself for no reason overhurriedly, forgetting – But *that* need not be spoken, I am unlikely ever to forget. How I did not feel the resulting difference in local temperature – how a stray draft or passing gust did not stir me to self-consciousness, I shall never truly know. The thing seems freakish. Perhaps the clemency of summer, perhaps the insufficient heating of my rented apartment – definitely my own self-departure. Kate Croy, therefore, is to blame. But, whatever, I disappeared, I appeared – the done cannot be undone, the undone done – I walked a distance, publicly and popularly, entered numerous 'shops', spoke to friends, acquaintances and was, as earlier noted, approached by kindly-meaning strangers. It was not until, sitting down for lunch, and placing as the consommé approached my napkin momentarily upon my lap, that I felt upon the back of my left hand a cold presence – unexpectedly tactile, neither cloth nor button, and, upon shocked examination, an intimate dependency. I shall never, I fear, never recover fully from the abysmal world-crushing soul-darkening terrification of that infinite moment. Had I – ? Surely – ? But then – ? And for – ? Not – ? Didn't I – ? That man – ? *Her* – ? All of them – ? It was enough to turn one instanter blubbing babe or quaking grandparent. In the ruins of all my former Corinth of pride, perhaps, the establishment of some future vestige of civilization, some few basic encampments, at that moment began – for I remained, at least, sane.

# The Sunflower

I am more than well aware of the current dilapidated banality of the *Metamorphosis*-genre: since Gregor Samsa awoke one morning having turned into what Nabokov – to whom I in all instances (excepting that of Dostoievskii) defer – insisted was *not* a cockroach, the genre has been in its definite decadence. After such mastery, such achievedness – what? What but imitation, failure, belittlement. A carnivalesque of Bloomian anxiety. Yet I was forced to concede to the necessity of telling when, one day, a year ago, the first shoot of what was in the fullness of its flowering to become a prime specimen of the genus *Helianthus* poked its green impertinence and terror out of my cheek, just in front of the left ear. If I could it would of course not have been that so-thoroughly-VanGoghed flower that I would have chosen to extrude. My prose, I realize (how I realize!), is but the polluted river resultant from several mighty tributaries – all of which should be more than obvious; but my cheek, surely an orchid, a narcissus, or even – oh God! – a simple pansy would have more accurately expressed me. For this was the first question necessary to be resolved: what sort of expression, if expression it was, was this? Was it my inward nature, my gauche unspoken loveliness, unable to escape through my mouth, therefore deciding on an exit point a few inches to the left? Or was it something external that had landed upon me – had I been seeded, impregnated, fertilized? – had some stray mutant spore somehow lodged itself in my jowl, rooted itself in my throat, and set forth its flower in the only place possible? Was this, in other words, expression or imposition, divinity or pure cruel accident?

The question unfortunately could not, at least as far as I could see, be resolved without the realm of the philosophic. But as I had no wish to become an axiom, I consulted no philosophers – and when they began publicly to theorize about the nature, or the unnature, of my 'condition' – microphones nestled gently on canapé-stained tweed; studio-lights, despite the best efforts of the make-up girl, transforming their naked pates into great fleshy viewer-repulsive mirrors; imitation leather sticky against the clenched intellectual buttock – when as I say the great, the good and the available at very short notice began their televisual odyssey through the absurd outer-wastes of the neo-Platonic, I did my best to avoid all cognizance of their solecisms. But that was in the later stages of the flowering of my face and of my fame; initially, I hid.

I went to the only place I could think of where my deformity, as I then thought it (the eight-page-spreads in the never-more-aptly-titled *The Face* being, as yet, undreamt), would be treated with discretion and, if possible, a slight measure of respect: The Holy Roman and Apostolic Church. As it happened, I had whilst at Oxford met a young probationary monk, with ginger hair and a weak contralto, named Brother O. He had

# DISCOVER THE BEST CUSTOMER SERVICES AT

# JOHN SMITH & SON

## B O O K S H O P S

57 ST. VINCENT STREET
GLASGOW G2 5TB
TEL: 0141 221 7472 FAX: 0141 248 4412
E-MAIL: 57@johnsmith.co.uk

### B O O K   O R D E R I N G
For any title not in stock

### B O O K   S E N D
To anywhere in the world

### B O O K   S E A R C H
For out of print titles

### B O O K   L I S T S
Provision of full bibliographic lists

### B O O K   S T A L L S
Exhibitions, fairs, conferences, lectures

### B O O K S   F O R   S C H O O L S
Set up school bookshops

### W E   A L S O   P R O V I D E
HMSO Agency for West of Scotland

Ordnance Survey Super National Agent
HSE Publications
Maps of the World
Foreign Newspapers & Magazines
Photocopying
Telephone Cards & Postage Stamps
Gift Vouchers
French, German, Spanish, Italian &
American Books-in-print
Computer Link to all Branches
Over 2 million Titles on our Database
An Offer to Order Multi-Media products
where possible

# JOHN SMITH & SON

**BOOKSHOPS**

# YOU'LL DISCOVER IT ALL

given me – one Michelmas term, over various herbal infusions – those few gentle strokings-of-the-trout that ephebe fishers of men try out on all their friends. Learning, he was, in that wonderful Catholic way, to play the long game: the patience, so truly named, of a saint. And now, after ten years, not long really, I was landed.

All it took was one phone call, a short and evasive explanation that there was something I couldn't explain over the phone; I was invited without hesitation up to Ampleforth. I drove through the night, up from coastal Cornwall, which was then my usual home. The black Jaguar was in a particularly sexy mood, groaning along the motorway, gasping at the audacity of my gear-changes. (A few of them even made me gasp.) On the way I had only one unwelcome sighting: whilst signing the light blue oblong tongue of the credit-card slip for some petrol at an open-all-nite service station, my face was momentarily exposed. The young man screamed, but then apologized.

'Speed?' I asked.

'Yes,' he said.

'Anything else?'

'A little acid.'

'Not good,' I said. 'Does funny things to the brain.'

The monks, bless them, took me in. Compared to a stigmatic, I was nothing to boast of. In fact, I was – for them – rather an ecumenical nightmare. The wounds of Christ, appearing even on an Irish housewife or Roumanian baby, were theological jackpot for their great Church of imitation and empathy, penitence and redemption, idolatry and superstition, appropriation and profit. But this sunflower-in-the-cheek business was equally if not more suitable to the gospel of Haight-Ashbury or of Greenpeace. The God revealed by my flower was impish, ironic, non-Theological, and even ('God' help us) post-Modern. Not Jehovah, certainly. And not Peter's Papal Pater. No doubt, in the privacy of their comfy cells, in between feasting, farting and flagellating, many of the monks regarded my growth as a work of the Devil. (It is not, I must admit, the first time myself or my adjuncts have been so considered.) The monastery as a whole, however, decided not to pass unnecessary and presumptuous judgment upon me, but to accept me as a bearer of at the most a unique affliction.

I did not, I must say, feel particularly afflicted. The horror of the first green outpoking passed with an almost incommunicable – because incredible – facility. I discovered on my left cheek a small reddish lumplet whilst shaving – which I assumed was one of those conscience-like early-to-mid-thirties pimples; I had in the immediate weeks been drinking too much and eating too richly, my complexion was moralizing: spotted face ergo spotted soul. So I bought a couple of bottles of mineral water and a dozen apples, walked the long way round the cliffs and returned all my overdue library books. None of which had any effect (except I never finished *Madness and Civilization*), for by the evening the quondam gentle bump had waxed to a bright purple protuberance, about the size and shape of the first join of my little finger. It hurt. It was the worst, most pullulant ulcer, the angriest zit, the most botched

injection – all at one and the same time. I tried dowsing
it with antiseptic fluids. I tried squeezing it. Then, as a
last mother-remembering superstition, I went to bed
and tried to forget all about it. But the hand *would* creep
up, unbidden, from the crutch to the cheek; the gothic
and fecund dark work its horrid alterations.

Slowly, through the frantic sleeplessness of that early
May night, I watched – at irregular intervals, sometimes
over an hour, sometimes less than a minute, always
excruciating – the purple turn grey, then black, then
green. Grey did not worry me particularly: I am often
turning grey; it is usually a sign that I am going to throw
up everywhere and immediately feel fine. Black, in a
way, I found quite pacifying: if things go black, they are
often about to shrivel up and drop harmlessly off. But
*green* – when a human body begins to turn green, it's a
certainty that something is seriously wrong. Green
brings with it deep primaevally nightmarish intimations
of chlorophyll – the terror of mere vegetable life.

'Conquer your fears, my child, eat your greens.'

'But, Mummy, I don't want to turn into a Brussels
sprout.'

(Perhaps I am reading too much subsequent thought
back into my initial reaction – but my first fear, as I
remember it, was not gangrene or syphilis, but some
new mutant chlorophyllic parasite, of which I was the
ground-breaking case; me, the monkey-fucker who gave
the world AIDS.)

Green means growth, that is its terror – and grow
it did.

But as it grew, over the following days and weeks,

I grew as well: I grew accustomed to it. I grew blasé. Not to the extent of going to a doctor or showing my face publicly, not that blasé, but intimately, in confab with the bathroom mirror, I soon came to accept that I had changed, and that my previously only sensed uniqueness was now manifesting itself physically.

The life of evasion and seclusion which I had immediately and almost with gratitude decided upon did not present me with any great psychic trauma. I was the definitive alumnus of the Glenn Gould School of Telephonic Friendship: I knew all their numbers, they did not know mine. My house was secluded, the mortgage paid off, and the furnishings as satisfactory as could be expected from people of that generation. Post, the little there was, got delivered to a visitable-at-unsociable-hours postal box. In a word, only the government could trace me; and I carefully gave them no reason for that. Food, I had delivered in a myriad of paper bags by the generic discrete little man from the shop in the next village. I made sure my trade was worth more to him than the prestige of being the source of fresh gossip. Money, had been adequately though one could never say lavishly provided by the unceasing and eventually mortal toil of my mother and father. (They died so my vocabulary might live.) What else? Sex – it was at first a bit of a problem, I must admit, but certain services can be procured even in the apparent hedonistic obscurity of Cornwall.

I suppose if I had wanted I could quite easily have continued on like this until death: my own or my flower's. But there was an inexplicable motive taking root in my being just as surely as the bloom was rooted in my face; the desire became overbiding to find myself (as I expressed it) a place in a 'community of the indifferent'. *Esse est percipi.* That was the motto which donged around in my brain throughout the month or two before the Ampleforth phone call. To be, for the Latinless, is to be perceived. Unseen, I felt myself to be imperceptibly fading; in sight, in soul. The shock of my Being, both in its floral manifestation and its tremulous imperceptibility – this must be experienced by others. I had a duty to perform toward both my essence and my physicality. Not wanting to cause a sensation, I must still be the cause of distinct individual sensations: light must reflect off me into the eyes of others; sounds I emit required the resonance of audition.

The question, the only awful question in your mind making that migrainey drum-drum-drum, is by now banging so loudly that even I, the previous and perhaps even posthumous writer, though by convention and all rationality deaf, can hear its distant future din. Let me therefore be merciful, if I can, and relieve you of it. Call down the spirits of Science and the ghosts of Healing to witness the Enquiry. Let eager Progress, suspicious Common Sense and fractious Curiosity have courtside seats. Let Humanity, wigged and gowned and slightly fuddled, preside. Let Persistence be prosecution, Reluctance defence. Be yourself the jury. Call the question forth!

'Why didn't you just go to the doctor?'

Why – why didn't I? Was it, perhaps, my fear of the

quiet scrubbed insatiable corridors, my disgust at the whored emotions and Auschwitz *politesse* of the meat-armed nurses, or my terror of the nice Doctor's hands, clean and wet and innocent as Pilate's? Did I dread being dissected as a curiosity or exhibited as a circus freak? Was I terrified of the psychologist's necrophilia, the physio-therapist's sadism, or the surgeon's rape? Was it merely the prospect of the waiting room with its alpine land-scapes, its moralizing guppies, its chatty syphilitic, its *time* – time sloppy and clotted, quease-making? Was it – could it simply have been the anxiety of travelling for the first time in weeks out of the house and to another acoustically-strange place? No – no to all of these. It was my sense of literary decorum which prevented me from entering the sensible world which you insist on inhabit-ing: my problem was not one of physiology, but of genre. I was in the wrong kind of story – the wrong kind of story was happening to me. For an aesthete such as myself, with the twilight inner tremulousness and dusky resonance of the late James – for such a one to be assaulted by the Gogolian absurd, the crass external-ization of the Kafkaesque: it was intolerable. My sensibility was of totally the wrong sort – this growth could do nothing, nothing but cheapen and worsen and vulgarize me.

Can you imagine what a doctor would have said, would have exclaimed, protested, opposed to all this – or worse, a head-shrinker: Freudian fuck-finder or Jungian sucker-for-symbols? Had I been able to consult Chekhov, something might have been done. But as it was I was unable to rely upon anyone but myself, or to depend upon any solutions but my own. At the time these solutions seemed quite obvious: an aesthetic problem demands an aesthetic solution. I must therefore find somewhere quiet and – uninterrupted – rewrite myself. Either in a more suitable if admittedly more vulgar genre, or, remaining my hothouse self, with another kind of blooming – lovely, internal, poignant. Always chivvied by a challenge, I decided on the latter. I must change the very inscription of my soul – if I succeeded, my face would follow; if not, then such abomination was unprecedented.

Whilst at Ampleforth, I became friends with a young novitiate whose name for his own protection was most definitely not Paul. Unable to adhere to the strict dialectic of the official orthodox attitude towards me: studied indifference mitigated by pastoral love – Paul came often to my secluded cell and asked me question after question. Here, in synecdoche, is the sort of conversation we really had – interspersed with what he touchingly considered diversionary chit-chat about Abbey power-politics, God, and Manchester United. (The latter a passion which, for our sins, we shared.)

'Do you feel ugly?'

'No, I feel absurd – quite a different thing.'

'Does it hurt?'

'Only if you touch it – then it explodes with pain.'

'Can I have a look inside your mouth?'

'Of course.'

'I can't see any roots. Do you think they've gone up into your brain?'

'If so, then my answer could hardly be expected to be objective: sunflower-mind-control would of course have me answer no. But I really truly don't have any idea. We could find out, but the x-ray solution must be retained until the last resort.'

'Do you feel closer to nature?'

'No. I feel imposed upon, not in any way organically similar. That I am a walking plant makes me, if anything, less natural than your average pedigree poodle.'

'Has it changed your attitude toward God?'

'Yes, I now suspect him even more of having some strange personal grudge against me. First my parents, then this! However, I have also entertained the poly-theistic possibility — this seems far more the imbecile prank of some piqued minor deity than the mighty work of the omniscient and all-forgiving Lord.'

'Why did you come here?'

'I do not require medical care, but some discrete gardening may — in the not too distant future — prove necessary.'

'Is this the first time something like this has happened to you?'

'No, last year it was a begonia and I joined the Hare Krishnas — of course it is!'

'Have you seen that painting by Van Gogh?'

'Paintings. Yes — unfortunately I have. I blame him as much as anybody.'

'Can I sit on your lap again, Daddy?'

And there, gentle reader, the door of discretion shuts — smooth and silent on obsequious hinges.

What then? Well, I flowered. This was about August. My seeds grew black and heavy. Movement soon became too great an agony, and I was confined – plantlike – to my bed. The seeds began to drop. Each was collected and numbered and labelled. The monastery gardener begged a clutch, to see if they would come up for him the following year. How could I refuse? But I made sure, before I gave him them, that he realized the risk he would be taking, and that I took no responsibility for what might happen. Several seeds which dropped off during the night were stolen by person or persons unknown. (Yes, they did feel like my children.) Shortly after which, news of my condition, now it was drawing to a close – retrospective proof being more recalcitrant than present – was discretely leaked to the Science Editor of *The Times*: the Church, I am sorry to say, wanted its pay-off. (What is it, in essence, but the biggest protection racket in history?) I decided therefore to cash in on myself myself. I was visited by distinguished scientists: botanists. Affidavits were procured. Professional hoax-crackers were turned, during brief examinations, from cynics to apostles. The tabloids began to brawl, financially-speaking, for exclusive access to the story of The Sunflower Man. The philosophers, one by one, eagerly took up the offer of a Warholean moment. *Vox pop* gasped, gulped, giggled. In fame, I met my proper apotheosis.

# Please Use a Basket

You know me, I'm the Boots *Please Use a Basket* girl. I stand beside the door in your local Boots, eight or ten of me, wire baskets stacked up to my tummy: unexceptionable, sisterly, happy to be of service; brunette, sparky-eyed, about 4' 9". The girl-next-door, only made out of cardboard. My nametag reads 'Mrs L. Timmins', but that's not my real name. My real name is Rebecca Llewellyn. You know me – you've probably even accepted my offer of a basket, once or twice. We know each other – we know each other well enough to ignore each other. Don't worry. I don't mind. I'll still be there the next time you shop with us: sisterly, brunette, about 4' 9". I will always be happy to be of service. Do you like the way I'm dressed? Do you like my white lab coatish uniform with its discreet navy trim? Does it make you trust me just that little bit extra, as if I were a doctor or a nurse? It should do – if it doesn't, there'll be hell to pay in Marketing. Because, you see, I'm not just a young woman called Rebecca Llewellyn; I'm not just that person who turned up to a photostudio in Battersea one July morning; I'm not just the daughter of Michael Llewellyn and Angela Sexton; I'm not just an image exposed onto Kodacolor Gold. I am a company policy decision. I am the ultimate expression of Boots' self-

image. I am a capitalistic device. You yourself must have
thought of it at least once. When you decide to *Please
Use a Basket*, you almost always end up buying more; if
only to kill the pathos of the single item in the vast
spatial yearning that is a Boots wire basket. (Wire for the
baskets is no accident, either: that simple grid provides
all the other customers with the exact co-ordinates of
your poverty.) It's simple, but it works. I must therefore
please, averagely. No one must find me in any way
offensive. (I have not yet mentioned that I am white –
but that is because you probably haven't even thought
about it. I must please the majority, and minorities are
called that for a reason. I am addressing an assumed
majority in which Mrs Smith outnumbers Mrs Patel –
an assumed majority in which Mrs Smith is white and
Mrs Patel isn't.) Perhaps I am not quite as nice as I at first
seem. Perhaps trustworthy young women like myself
were employed in certain places half a century ago. You
know me, I'm the Auschwitz *Please Remove Your Clothes*
girl: unexceptionable, sisterly, happy to be of service;
brunette, sparky-eyed, about 4' 9". A little like Uncle
Michael and Aunt Angela's daughter, Rebecca. Only
made out of cardboard. And now you think I have
ruined my point by overstating it. And I probably have.
But the problem with fascism is, according to some, that
it can only accurately be called fascist when it is no
longer any use to call it anything. When I joined the
SWP, about a year after that July morning in Battersea,
I didn't realize the true threat of fascism. I was coming
out of Boots one evening after work. All day I had been
on the checkout with Marge and Mavis. Even though

I'd dyed my hair cherry and changed it to a really short bob, people still recognized me as the *Please Use a Basket* girl. 'It's you, isn't it? Over there – it's you.' The young woman selling the Socialist Worker was just like me – brunette, sparky-eyed, about 4' 9" – only she wore vegetarian Docs, calico and a Donkey Jacket where I wore Clarks, a lab coatish uniform and a Debenham's raincoat. She smiled at me, in between shouts. I bought one of her newspapers, though I really wasn't sure what it was. We started having a really good chat. I told her how fed up I was, working at Boots. We went for a coffee. I told her I was the Boots *Please Use a Basket* girl. She called me a 'tool of the capitalist hegemony'. She explained what hegemony meant. Instantly, I recognized that she was telling the truth. She had the forms with her, so I signed up. What I'd realized was that, if anyone else was to change, if the capitalist hegemony was ever going to be smashed, then the Boots *Please Use a Basket* girl had to be in the vanguard. I had been selected, selected from hundreds, as an image acceptable to the masses. I myself had been mass-produced – there were now literally masses of me. I was a crowd, a mob, an army. But I was an army lined up against myself. I was the fascist oppressor – but I knew that I was made of cardboard and that I couldn't speak. Rebecca Llewellyn now began her campaign against the Boots *Please Use a Basket* girl. I resigned from Boots, after seven years, sending a letter of explanation to all the senior management. 'Your cardboard representative, your ubiquitous symbol of hegemony is now against you,' I wrote. 'You have created me till I outnumbered you.' Nancy helped me with the letter. Nancy is the name of the girl who sold me my first copy of the Socialist Worker. We live together in a Battersea squat, just round the corner from the photostudio. We go on rallies and demos together. Last year we went on the big anti-fascist march round the East End and got into a fight with Combat 18 and the BNP. We also went to Reading and Glastonbury. Nancy's lovely. Her regular patch is by the tube station; mine's outside the Boots where the old Rebecca Llewellyn used to work. So now, even as I stand inside, warm under fluorescent light, eight or ten of me – *Please Use a Basket, Please Use a Basket, Please Use a Basket, Please Use a Basket, Please Use a Basket, Please Use a Basket, Please Use a Basket, Please Use a Basket, Please Use a Basket, Please Use a Basket* – I also stand outside, alone, in the weather, shouting, 'Socialist Worker! Socialist Worker! Socialist Worker! Socialist Worker! Socialist Worker! Socialist Worker! Socialist Worker! Socialist Worker! Socialist Worker! Socialist Worker!' And no one recognizes me anymore.

# Fluffy Pink Bunny Rabbit

Let me tell you why I stopped being an actor.

I'd just finished a short but well received run, in *Vanya*, in Edinburgh and London. There were, because of that, a few things in the air that hadn't quite firmed up yet.

'Take a week or two off,' my agent said. 'You deserve it.'

But, spendthrift that I am, the *Vanya* money had already vamoosed. Suffice to say, I was distinctly unliquid.

My daughter, Sally, was coming up to her fifth birthday. Presents, and a school uniform, and perhaps also a school, were required. My wife, Kate, was doing what she could – which was supply teaching, which kept a roof.

It has rightly been said of the acting profession, 'One week you're Macbeth, the next McBurglar.' I didn't stoop that low – I stooped much much lower.

A friend of a friend, name of Bob, told me – during that friend's dinner party – about a gig shaking tins for a children's cancer charity. (To avoid offence, I'll just call it 'The Children's Cancer Charity'.) The job was mentioned in a 'who'd be desperate enough to take that' kind of way. I laughed and said, 'God, yes!' Unfortunately, Kate overheard and cornered me in the kitchen.

'Take it,' she said.

I went back to Bob and got the number. I said I had a
friend who might be interested.

But the following Friday, when I turned up at the
Children's Cancer Charity offices to collect my gear,
who was waiting there but Bob?

'So, you're that desperate, as well?' I said.

'Fuck, yeah,' he said.

There were about six other men there. I recognized
two of them from that year's fringe productions. I think
one of them did physical theatre. We avoided eye contact.

The gear consisted of:

    10 collecting tins
    2,000 Children's Cancer Charity stickers
    1 rabbit suit, in fluffy pink
    1 rabbit suit head, pink and fluffy
    1 map of assigned locations

A stern-but-caring-looking woman, Mrs Hopkinson,
briefed us. We were to do seven hours a day. This would
last a week, Monday to Friday. The better-paid weekend
positions had already gone. We would have to return the
costumes on Friday evening. She would come along a
couple of times each day to collect our hopefully filled-
up tins. Competition for the job was tough, so quitters
weren't what they were looking for. She paused to allow
quitters to quit. Bob, I and the others all sat firm. I'd
swallowed my pride the week before, when I made the
initial phone call, so it had been shat out and flushed
down the pan days ago.

The woman told us finally:

'If it ever gets tough, and it will, and you feel like

stopping smiling or shaking your tin that little less ardently, just think of the children – think of their faces. You're doing this for them.'

Bob and I, having secured the gig, repaired, in the time-honoured fashion, to a local hostelry – where we began to discuss our roles and spend our unearned riches.

As he was getting the bitters in, I asked him:

'Have you ever done anything like this before?'

'A friend told me the trick is to travel to the gig in costume.'

'Oh, yes?'

'Well, it saves having to find somewhere to stow your stuff.'

'Or get changed.'

'Exactly.'

We agreed to meet up each day for lunch. Two men dressed as fluffy pink bunny rabbits were, if anything, slightly less ridiculous than one. We contemplated our costumes, as they lay at our feet on the carpet. So this was failure.

'Where can we go? Not a pub, surely.'

'No. You might want to go back there,' said Bob. 'McDonald's – I don't think they'd even notice.'

The Charity was giving us only a small lunch allowance, so boozing it up probably wasn't a good idea. It might help with the smiling and shouting, but the shaking would go all to pot.

Bob was from Scotland, and had once played Malcolm in an all-nude production of *Macbeth*. It was the high point of his career – in all senses of the word. Since then

he had mainly played thugs and social workers. He'd
never done Chekhov.

I didn't really like Bob all that much – mostly because
I had the distinct feeling he'd tell everybody about this
particular low point in my career (if not immediately,
then when I was famous) – but he did have *one* good
point: a mobile phone. This meant that I could at least
give my agent a number. I could also phone my wife –
to ask if my agent had called.

'Why are you doing jobs like this if you can afford
one of those?' I asked, as we waited on Oxford Street for
my bus.

'I did a promotion for them,' Bob said. 'Anyway, costs
more to get rid of the bloody thing than to keep it.'

The bus arrived.

I got on, the bunny head hitting the floor as I lunged
for my change. I received my first funny look from the
driver.

'See you Monday,' said Bob.

○

That evening, back home in Chiswick, I tried on the
bunny suit. Sally, of course, loved it.

'Hop, Daddy, hop!' she shouted, as I padded into the
kitchen.

And being that kind of dad, I hopped and hopped and
hopped until it was way past her bedtime. The downstairs neighbours only complained once.

'Rabbit must be hungry,' she said, just as I'd tucked
her in. So, to the kitchen we went – Sally insisting on

feeding me some carrots before she went to sleep. It was all I could do to stop her going out into the backstreets of Chiswick to find some hay for my hutch.

Back in the master bedroom, Kate told me she found the whole get-up was making her feel 'mysteriously horny'. The suit's zip ran down the side, so I had to take it off before we had sex.

'At it like bunny rabbits,' Kate said, afterwards.

We both had to bite the duvet to keep from waking Sally.

Much of the night was spent exchanging 'my-widdw-fwuffy-bunny'-type endearments.

○

On the Monday morning, Kate and Sally waved me off.

'Did you still got your carrots, Mr Rabbit?' asked Sally.

I picked the pink lunchbox out from among the collecting tins and stickers in my plastic bag. Sally had been quite insistent that she and Mummy make this up for me.

In Sally's little world, I'd stopped being Daddy and had become Mr Rabbit – even when I no longer had the costume on. The metamorphosis had begun when I first put the costume on, on Friday evening. By Saturday lunchtime, she was insisting I eat nothing but carrots and asking to stroke me at every opportunity. By Sunday morning, she became very miffed if ever I forgot to hop around the flat – even when I demonstrated to her how it was almost impossible to hop with a bowl of corn-flakes in your hands.

'Come back safe, my fwuffy bunnikins,' said Kate, and gave me a kiss.

One of the downstairs neighbours walked by.

'What's up, Doc?' he said.

○

I took the tube in to Piccadilly Circus, the first location on my map. Bob had a cushy start, having copped for Covent Garden.

In order to have something else to concentrate on during the journey, I took a book. In the midst of all Kate's bunny-jokes, she had started singing:

> Run, rabbit
> Run, rabbit
> Run, run, run...

We had an old orange Penguin copy of Updike's *Rabbit, Run* which I'd bought for 30p in Oxfam and never read. I decided I'd either have to get into the spirit of the bunny-punning or go mad – I also didn't mind if it got nicked.

I sat with my head beside me on the next seat, trying to read. The head kept rolling off. Eventually, I put it on my lap.

People looked, then looked away, then looked back, then stared, then looked away, then looked back.

A couple of wags, just before they got off, whispered, 'What's up, Doc?' But, to be honest, they seemed much more embarrassed than I did. Only one person laughed, and I couldn't tell if that was at me or at something the person with them had said.

Even so, I didn't manage to read very much. Updike's novel was all in the present tense, which made me feel rather queasy.

When we got to Piccadilly, I stowed the book in the plastic bag, picked my head up by the ears and joined the crowd for the stairs.

I was as nervous as I could remember being since my RADA graduation show.

○

For the first couple of hours, I didn't actually mind the work too much. I was getting through the stickers at a fair lick, though I was sure the tin was full of coppers. The morning was mild, so I didn't get too sweaty in the bunny costume – its collar had already begun to chafe against my neck. I had people's attention, and I always like that. What was best about it was the children. They all loved me as much as Sally had. In fact, I'm sure my meagre takings would have been even meagerer had not the little darlings come to my rescue. I watched them with love as they tugged on sleeves, whispered into downbended ears and slyly sidled over with fistfuls of sweaty change. Placing the stickers on their pullovers and sweatshirts was like pressing a button marked, 'Beamy smile.' They knew what I wanted, even if they didn't know what I wanted it for. I was rather worried about this, so as soon as I saw a child approaching, I stopped shouting, 'Children's Cancer Charity!' and reverted to the anodyne, 'Please give generously!' The thought of one of the little things going back to their parents and saying, 'Mummy, what's cancer?' — well, it wasn't something that was going to happen if I could help it.

○

Bob was already halfway through his second Cheeseburger when I got to the Oxford Street McDonald's. (We'd arranged to meet inside, downstairs.) His head and collecting tin were lying unembarrassedly on the table.

'What's up, Doc?' he inquired, semi-ceremonially, as I sat down beside him in the piney alcove.

I couldn't come up with a witty reply, so I just ate.

My solitary Big Mac contained too much onion and not enough gherkin. My fries were crystalline with salt and my Coke was watery. I anticipated an afternoon of thirst.

'Just think of the children's faces,' I said, eventually.

'Concentrate on it,' said Bob.

'Focus.'

I looked round at some of the children at the other tables. Some of them looked back. I looked at their faces, trying to fix them in my noddle. A little girl came over and put a pound coin in Bob's tin. Bob didn't even look at her.

I tried phoning my agent, but just got her VoiceMail.

'I saw Jonathan Miller,' Bob said.

'Did he give you anything?'

'No.'

'Tight bastard.'

'I wanted to speak to him,' said Bob, 'but he'd've known I was an out-of-work actor, wouldn't he?'

'Would he?'

'Of course. You don't get brickies or school teachers dressed in bunny costumes.'

I thought about this for a while. It was probably true, though school teacher Kate had tried on the costume just for fun.

○

In the afternoon, the sun came out and I began to sweat.

I was menaced by a couple of cidered-up skinheads, and rescued by a pair of London's finest constabulary.

'What's up, Doc?' they said.

''Ello, 'ello, 'ello,' I replied.

By the evening, my throat was trashed and, when I got home, I wasn't going to play Mr Rabbit for anyone – not even the pleading Sally.

'Mr Rabbit wants some carrot,' she said.

'No,' I said, 'Mr Rabbit wants some Scotch.'

Sally watched disapprovingly as I tucked in to pasta and pesto.

'She wanted to come and see you,' said Kate, after Sally had gone tearfully to bed.

'God,' I said, '*no.*'

'I agreed to take her at the end of the week – on your last day. We'll take the tube in and go with you to McDonald's for lunch.'

'Oh, that'll be a treat,' I said.

'It will for her. Where are you on Friday?'

'Trafalgar Square.'

That night, we didn't have sex. The bunny suit was made of some cheap acrylic which over the days left a smell on my skin like burnt matches. Kate said it made her feel ill.

○

Monday. Piccadilly Circus. £93.56

   Tuesday. Regent Street. £86.89

   Wednesday. Tottenham Court Road. £95.34

○

Thursday lunchtime. McDonald's. After I'd finished on his phone, Bob said he was thinking about giving up.

'I can't take any more of it. I should be doing *Hamlet*, *Peer Gynt*, *Vanya* – '

'Careful,' I said, 'you're starting to sound like an actor.'

'Snivelling child molester in *The Bill*, even. I'm serious.'

'Think of their faces.'

'I can't anymore. I'm thinking that I smell so bad Richard won't come near me, I'm thinking that my neck is raw as fuck, I'm thinking that I've seen five people I know – '

'What did they say?'

'Guess.'

'It's awful when you learn your friends aren't capable of anything more than all the other sad unfunny bastards.'

Bob didn't answer. He was drawing triangles in his ketchup with a french fry.

I'd seen four acquaintances, but managed to avoid being recognized by three of them.

'You'll go on, though, won't you? We'll have a drink, Saturday night, when we've had a day to recover.'

'I suppose so,'

'Come on, mate.'

○

Thursday. Oxford Street. £104.08

Did it! I cracked the ton.

○

Friday. Trafalgar Square.

(I bloody hate Trafalgar Square. I went on three school trips during my entire education, and they all involved the National Gallery and Trafalgar Square. I hate pigeons. I hate tourists. I hate Nelson's Column. I hate having my photo taken dressed as a fluffy pink bunny. For some reason, the tourists flocked to me like – pigeons. I decided to start charging them a quid a snapshot. If the punks across the way could do it, so could I.)

Although I'd pretended to be against it, I found I was looking forward to Sally's visit from the moment I got there.

'You didn't let her see me in *Vanya*,' I'd said to Kate, the night before. 'She's going to remember me as a fluffy pink rabbit.'

'No, she won't.'

'I was proud of myself for once. I was where I should be.'

'God, don't you just go on about it?'

'But it was what I got into this whole thing for.'

'We need the money. You'll have stopped smelling by Sunday.'

'I bloody hate myself.'

'Join the club.'

We had slept on the argument and didn't make up in the morning. Kate was in no mood for rabbit jokes when I left, though Sally still insisted I take my lunch-box. I hadn't been getting on with Updike, so bought a *Guardian* for the last day.

'What's up, Doc?' said the newsagent.

It got to one o'clock, and I started to look out for Kate and Sally even more.

I was hoping that getting together for lunch with Sally would bring Kate and me back on terms.

A Japanese couple gave me a fiver for a photo.

Running through the crowd, sending off a wave of pigeons, came a man dressed as a pink rabbit. It took me a moment to remember that I knew him, that it was Bob, and that I was also dressed as a pink rabbit. He was clutching his mobile phone. There was a very strange look about him – the look rabbits get when your headlights tell them they are going to die. I was certain it was because my agent had just got me a very good part.

Bob stopped in front of me.

'You've got to go to the hospital. St Thomas'. Over the river.'

'What?'

'There's been an accident.'

'Sally!' I cried.

'No,' he said, 'Kate.'

'What?'

'She went under a tube train. Don't know how it happened.'

'Oh God,'

'She's okay, they think.'

'She didn't phone you herself?'

'The hospital found my number on her.'

I remembered writing it out for her on a Post-it note.

'Will you come?' I asked.

'Take a taxi,' he said.

'But I haven't – '

'Bust open the tin. I'm sure they'll understand.'

○

I caught a cab at the side of the square.

'What's up, Doc?' said the cabbie.

'St Thomas' Hospital, please,' I said. 'As quickly as possible.'

'Wife having bunnies, is she?' joked the cabbie.

'No, my wife may be dying.'

I tugged off the rabbit head and placed it on the seat beside me. The cab pulled out in front of a cab. We drove down Whitehall.

'That myxomatosis, eh?' joked the cabbie. 'Terrible this time of year, innit?'

'I'm serious,' I said.

'Why are you got up like that then?'

'Please, for Christ's sake, just shut up.'

I glanced at the back of the cabbie's head. For a moment, it seemed to me that he was completely constructed from the thousands of Full English Breakfasts he had eaten. The back of his neck was streaky bacon. His ears were huge mushrooms. His hair was an accumulation of every hair I'd ever picked out of my food. In the rear view mirror, I saw his fried bread forehead, his grilled tomato mouth, his black pudding chin, his pork sausage nose.

I couldn't tell whether it was the taxi or my stomach that lurched.

I didn't have time to reach the window, so I picked up my bunny head and puked into that.

'Oh, stag night, was it?' the Full English Breakfast said, unconcerned. I immediately wished I'd hurled behind the fold-down seat – without him noticing.

I balanced the head between my feet. My vomit really *was* full of diced carrot.

'Did you have any bunny girls there?'

I tried to open the collecting tin, but my hands were muffled by the pink mittens. I unzipped the side of the costume, pulled down the top half. My T-shirt and boxers were sodden. I got my nails through the tamper-proof sticker. The tin contained more than enough.

'Sorry for rabbiting on.'

We were crossing Westminster Bridge, almost there. I saw a couple of nurses, out on their lunch break. I noticed their uniforms.

'Nice place, that Watership Down.'

I realized that I hadn't been trying hard enough not to think of Kate. Then I realized I hadn't been thinking of Kate at all.

The cab stopped outside the front gates.

I paid, and the Full English Breakfast undid the central locking.

'Have a nice day,' he said.

'Cunt,' I said.

○

I hurried into Casualty, carrying my fluffy pink head full of orange vomit. I knew that if I chucked it away, I would be charged for losing the whole costume. That would probably be an excuse for them not to pay me; whereas, I could always wash the head and return it. I was sure it wouldn't smell any worse than it already did. These were half my thoughts.

At the Enquiries Desk, I asked under my wife's name. The man directed me to Intensive Care.

I began to run, skimming past orderlies with wash-buckets and old men in dressing gowns. I got lost. I asked directions. I walked through yet another set of white swing doors.

There was another reception. I gave my name.

'It's my wife.'

The nurse looked at my costume, smelt my head.

'I was collecting for charity,' I explained.

'She's in Bed 9.'

'Children's Cancer Charity,' I said, holding up the

violated collecting tin. I realized I didn't have my stickers with me. Nor my copy of the *Guardian*.

'I'll take you,' the nurse said.

'Hold on,' I said.

I stood there for a moment, looking at myself through her eyes: a man, dressed as a pink fluffy bunny rabbit; a man whose wife was critically ill. I thought about asking her for some clothes, a dressing gown, anything.

'Your daughter's with her, I think.'

'Bed 9, you say?'

I could hear the nurse trotting after me.

'Slow down!' she shouted.

Bed 9 was on the left, at the end. Kate was there — tubes in her nose, out of her arms. Sally sat next to the bed, holding her mother's hand. A man in a white coat was checking on one of the monitors. There was the bip-bip-bip of Kate's heartbeat. The nurse caught up. Kate was wearing a disposable nightdress. The nurse spoke to the man in the white coat.

'It's her husband,' she said.

Sally turned and looked at me for the first time.

'Mr Rabbit,' she said.

The man in the white coat stepped towards me.

'Mr Evans,' he said.

'Hello, Mr Rabbit,' said Sally.

I dropped my head onto the floor and saw some of the vomit slip out.

'What's up, Doc?' I asked, and then collapsed.

# "Polly"

"Polly" is still stable. Her obs are fine. Her pulse rate is okay, 190 or so — which is a little faster than we'd like. Blood pressure doesn't vary much from 50/25. Respirations are 40. Oxygenation is improving. Arterial gas levels are normal: $CO_2$ at 5, $O_2$ at 21%. She is keeping, with assistance, a good steady temperature of 37° C. Electrolytes are fine. She looks well hydrated. Her Coma Score hasn't moved. Still no motor responses, spontaneous noises, response to pain, etc.

I've just changed her.

The police have almost completed their enquiries.

It's almost hard to look at her, she's so perfect-looking. At this time of night, there's only the lamps pointed to the wall and a little light from the monitors. She looks bluey-green, as if the incubator was a fishtank. But there's red in the reflections. You can't see much of her, for all the tubes and tape, but by now I know how she looks and feels. She has a very hard body for a baby, very muscular, though her muscles have started to atrophy. Her elbows are very sharp. She's put on a little, but she still weighs only 3.28 kg. She has blue eyes, like you'd choose for a child if you could, but they don't open. Her hair is blonde, though that could change later. It did with me. She'd never be a redhead is about all we can tell for definite. There is a mole shaped like nothing-in-particular on her abdomen. At the moment it's hidden by the UVC. Looks like I'll have to flush that out later. Her face is quite long and thin for a newborn.

When she came in, she was dehydrated and hypo-thermic. This had led to acidaemia and hypoxaemia. There were also serious problems with her respiration. Perinatal asphyxia was suspected.

The doctor said the damage was already irreversible.

"Polly" was found (she really *was*) by 'a man out walking his dog'. What he was doing walking it through the graveyard, when there's a perfectly good park not two streets away, I have no idea. "Polly" was lying on the grave – the man told me, and I went back and checked – of one 'Griselda Quesne / 1818–1857 / A precious flower / garner'd by God.' (It was in the local papers. They called her 'The Graveyard Girl', which I didn't like at all. It made her sound ghoulish.) We decided not to call her Griselda. It was suggested that leaving a baby in a grave-yard seemed a bit of a literary thing to do. The police have been making enquiries at the university. "Polly" was wrapped in a red and black tartan blanket, stuffed into a Fyffes banana box. The police have been making enquiries at all the local grocers. Because of 'Fyffes', we thought of calling her 'Fiona' or 'Fi-fi', for short. (Someone also suggested 'Nana' from 'ba-nana'.) In the end, we – I, actually – called her "Polly", after the dog the man was out walking. Polly is a stubby-tailed Jack Russell, with a yap that is endearing for about five

minutes. (I'm a cat person, myself. Jason wants a dog.)
As she hates anything in a uniform (she was abducted
from a dustbin to Battersea Dog's Home), her hours in
the hospital did not pass in silence. She succeeded in
getting her teeth into one of the porters. He had to sit in
a wheelchair in Casualty, waiting for a porter – which
gave us all a laugh. Polly's owner told us her history, in
great detail, again and again. But she *did* save a life – and
how many can claim to have done that? (Apart from
those of us whose job it is.) According to the doctor,
"Polly" was born less than 8 hours before being found.
That makes her a Virgo, like me. Her umbilical cord had
been cut about six inches along, sealed off with some
multicoloured rubber bands. Forensics are analysing
these at the moment. The police have been making
enquiries at all the local stationers. The fact they were
multicoloured does suggest, a bit worryingly, that "Polly"
belongs to a young girl – someone still at school, even.
The police have been making enquiries at local schools.
Late shift gives you time to think about these things. It's
hard to imagine how you keep a pregnancy secret from
your family and schoolfriends. Perhaps, for "Polly's"
mother, there was one friend who knew, who helped.
Who was there at the birth with the scissors. Who
thought of the rubber bands. Perhaps who even took
"Polly" to the graveyard and left her there. The police
have been making enquiries among local residents.

Sometimes a case – just like all the others – for some silly
reason hooks into your heart and starts to pull chunks of
it away. We get moved around, a different baby every

shift, but you still have your favourites. I think, in "Polly's" case, it was the Ffyfes box. (Two bananas were still in the bottom of the box, under the blanket, under the baby.) And even though you *know* you shouldn't let the whole thing happen again, you do: if only to prove to yourself that you can still feel something other than frustration about your work, about the politics of it all. Usually it's seeing the parents makes you feel this way. The babies are okay. The babies are just doing their own thing, trying their best to live. But the parents come in with such amazing hope. The Caucasians are the worst for accepting when their baby is going to die. 'But you can do anything these days,' they say. The Bangladeshi women just say, 'It is the will of Allah.' But "Polly" has been more than just another case from the moment I saw her — her floppy grey little body. I was half way through my shift when she arrived. We resuscitated her, intubated her, put her in an incubator. An hour or so later, I performed the umbilical artery catheterization. Perhaps it's also to do with skipping my last month's period, thinking I was pregnant. Luckily, I didn't tell Jason — and he didn't notice — he would either have been delighted or walked. We haven't been going out that long. Three months, eight days. We haven't discussed babies. He works for the council. He's a Leo; I'm a Virgo. We're not meant to be that compatible. We get along okay, though he wants to go out and do things more than I do. He's cuspal, though — so I have hopes.

That was the Registrar just went past.

I don't know why, but I went out on my last day off and

had a horoscope done for "Polly". It seemed the closest thing I could do to giving her a personality, a life.

"Polly" came in a couple of weeks ago, on a Wednesday, at 5 in the afternoon. If the doctor was right, that means she was born around 9 a.m. Her mother must have been in labour overnight.

So, assuming she was born at 8.30 (doctors usually get things a little wrong) and on a latitude and longitude not too far from the graveyard, it means we can cast quite an accurate astrological chart for her. That's what I thought, anyway.

A woman on the Market Square did it for me. I didn't really feel qualified enough myself, though I often get books out of the library. I told her my estimated date and time and place of birth. I didn't tell her about "Polly's" particular circumstances.

She posted me a computer printout a couple of days later. It's in my bag. I thought about taping it to the outside of her incubator, but I'm sure the doctors would think it a silly, nursey kind of thing to do.

I might still show it to Jason.

This is what "Polly's" horoscope says:

Congratulations on the birth of your child!
As a typical Virgo, Polly will be loyal, kind, quiet, modest, loving, perfectionist, diplomatic, shy.
Virgoes are artistic and creative, but not as strong with the use of words as they are with using pictures. Virgoes are great perfect people to have around in a crisis. Virgo friendships are something they will never give lightly, but once they give it,

it will stay firm through thick and through thin.
If Virgos have a weakness, it is for self-indulgence
in their emotions. Expect sulks from a Virgo child
and arguments with an adolescent. Virgos can be
very introspective but secretly play-acting people
– and they are very bad for bearing grudges.
But they do appreciate honesty, so be honest with
her. Virgos are among the underachievers of this
world, tending to find private rather than public
success. Virgos, as an Earth sign, are most compatible with these other signs, Capricorns and
Taureans. Virgos are most incompatible with
Leos and Sagittarians.

For this particular Virgo, Polly, the stars hold
much of promise. Polly will be a lively and
intelligent child. A little shy and not pushful.
Doing well at school, with widespread interests,
particularly in artistic subjects. Polly will enjoy
handicrafts and music, and may pursue this as a
career. She will be shy of boys until later than
other girls, but I forsee some four or five shorter
relationships before Mr Right comes along. He
will be a dominent Pisces. They will have two or
three children. Polly will have a successful
independent career as a woman of the next
millennium. If she has any health problem it will
situate in the bowels. Polly will live to a ripe old
age, keeping her youthful appearance

# IYouHeSheItWeYouThey

*Und jene, die schön sind, / o wer hält sie zurück?*
And those who are beautiful / oh who can retain them?
— Rilke, *Second Duino Elegy*

Understand me — physical beauty isn't the problem and never has been: 6' 4" — Pale — Byronic — Hung.

(I was once flown out to Tokyo to do a show for *Dolce & Gabbana*. Schoolgirls mobbed me from Customs to catwalk and back, putting sweeties in my *Paul Smith* pockets.)

I'm cute. Helplessly cute. This isn't, like, vanity; this is a fact. People pay me for how I look. To see me is to want to shag me — and that counts for both sexes: hetero or homo.

The problem is this: when I find someone cute *myself*, I immediately begin to mumble and to fumble — when I *desire* someone, I just make a run for the door — but when I desire someone really *passionately*, I faint.

Dead. Completely. Sorry.

Often, at the exact moment of orgasm, I lose consciousness; but also, now and again, when my desire is passionate and immediate, I can flake out while simply being introduced:

'Gabriel, this is Blanka; Blanka, *Gabriel?*'

I was lucky not to have fainted the moment Blanka entered the room. (The room was a Soho loft; the moment was 11.47 p.m., New Year's Eve, 1994.)

Someone took Björk's *Debut* off the CD player and put on Portishead's *Dummy*.

Watching the world turn dangerously polka dot, I grasped the glassy edge of the dining room table. I concentrated on the middle candle of the black iron candelabra. 'Tat from *Habitat*,' I thought, and the thought, for the moment, saved me.

Getting ready to go out that evening, slinking into my *Armani*, I felt I was fairly safe from humiliation: loss of consciousness is pretty *de rigueur* on New Year's Eve, doubly so in Soho.

A Vivienne Westwood regular, Blanka, as well as being faint-makingly gorgeous (and I know gorgeous pretty much backwards) was also slightly – no, *more* than slightly – scarifying.

Above the endearing Bambi-on-stilts swingsway of Blanka's supermodel legs, that famous upper body moved with the semi-Fascist precision of a self-acknowledged Aryan. 6' 3" – Golden – Snowy – Stacked: Blanka made everyone else at the party feel Semitic.

Two of the actual Jews, writers, seeing Blanka enter, left almost immediately. That was Blanka's constant effect: pogrom.

'Gabriel, this is Blanka etc.'

I am, of course, Jewish. By making the introduction, our host, Christopher, was hoping Blanka and I would sort of racially neutralize one another. Instead, I desired,

I fainted, and, as I later found out, even more people started to leave.

'Just going to Trafalgar, darling. Rub my body against the sweaty masses. That sort of thing. Chow-chow.'

When I came round I found I had been moved through into the bedroom. I had been there before, with several of Christopher's friends at several of Christopher's parties. As there was no light on, the room was illuminated by the orange gloom that loomed outside.

Christopher, a dancer, thought I was gay – and I let Christopher go on thinking I was gay, though I knew I wasn't.

That didn't mean I didn't put out. For a while, I was a right little trollop. With men, luckily, I didn't faint so often. I like being around for when I come or at least when someone else does.

Looking up through the glass roof, I could see fuzzy-brown mizzle-distance where the stars were meant to be.

I like the stars, but I don't get a chance to see that kind of thing that often. Stars stop me feeling lonely.

Christopher wasn't into furniture: bed, bedside table, wall wardrobe, strobe lamps. All new, all white.

Apart from the coats and bags, which were now on the floor, the bedroom was straight out of *Interiors* circa 1984. Post-Minimalism Revisited. A chi chi cliché.

My waking hope, I have to admit, was that Blanka wouldn't be there when I looked round –

'Gabriel?' Blanka had been sitting on the edge of the bed, chin on her knees.

'Yes.'

'Gabriel, I'm sorry – '

'No, *I'm* sorry – '

'But I – '

'Really, no: I fainted, not – '

'Yes, but that – '

'Forget – '

'Sorry – '

When I kissed Blanka, I wanted to stop this stupid-stupid conversation. (The fact that New Year was striking was completely irrelevant. Or almost completely.) Unfortunately, the conversation was to continue, just as stupid, for the rest of the year.

○

– You're so fucking selfish. You never think of anyone or anything but your own fucking self. Nothing but you-you-*you*-you-you. You lie there in your bed wearing your stupid mumsey stripey pyjamas with your *Premiere* and your *Playboy* and you don't do a thing all day. What do you do, then? What *do* you do? How do you make any valid contribution to the world? You just take-take-take. You never give anything back. Drinking Diet Coke and watching M-fucking-TV. Gabriel, are you listening? You better be listening! Take that fucking pillow off your head! *Gabriel*. Gabriel! Fucking get into your fucking head what's fucking going on!

– Swear a bit more, Blanka, why don't you?

– You think that's smart? You think you're a real witty little wanker, don't you?

– No, but you seem to.

– You arrogant bastard.

– And you're not?

– You're Adolf-fucking-Hitler, you –

– And you're Eva-fucking-Hitler-fucking-Braun –

– You're an arsehole. A complete arsehole.

– Which is better, you'll admit, than an incomplete –

– You *listen*. Alright? You just listen. You take your poncey books –

– Nietzsche is *not* poncey –

– and your poncey CDs and –

– Wagner *isn't* –

– your poncey wok and your shoes –

– So the shoes aren't poncey?

– Everything about you is poncey. You – *ponce!*

– Okay – carry on.

– Take your poncey guitar, which you can't even fucking play –

– Can't play?

– your stupid boring Damien Hirst –

– Jimi Hendrix –

– your –

– Jimmy Page –

– plants and shit and your –

– Johnny Marr –

– Stop that, Gabriel!

– Dwoaaow-kkchingk-dwaow-dwaow!

– Gabriel –

– Bweeeeiiii-aeiou-zzzzz-nnnnn!

– *Gab* –

– What?

– Get out!

And that was only January.

○

Gabriel didn't really work. He didn't need to. His family did the money thing. He was very beautiful, so people forgave him almost anything. He liked to think of himself as an actor, though he'd never been onstage, or as a writer, though he never got past page three. (Page four is the difficult one, as all *real* writers know.) He'd done some modelling once, but not much more than catalogues. There was something very stiff about him. He just didn't photograph as well as he should. On the catwalk, he couldn't move so the clothes looked good. And then, his hair was always the right length one month too late. The agency dropped him after six haircuts. His portfolio dropped into the Thames. He dropped most of his friends. (Among which ... )

So, despite being so exceptionally good-looking, Gabriel never really got anywhere. He was a very successful failure and a very prominent nobody. Until he met Blanka. Blanka made a big difference in Gabriel's life. Oh, Blanka – Blanka, Blanka, *Blanka* – Gabriel didn't know what he was letting himself in for. (Several people might have told him. Mentioning no names. Blanka had been on the scene a while. Blanka was *known*.)

Gabriel was a complete innocent.

He'd grown up in 'a leafy suburb more leafy than suburban'. His father was an Investment Broker and his mother was a Merchant Banker. Gabriel's younger brother, Michael, was going to be an Investment Banker. (Unfortunately, that wasn't a joke.)

His parent's biggest indulgence was entering themselves for ludicrously high-calibre bridge tournaments.

At school he was always in the team but never in the action. At university he was always in the action but never in the mood. In India he was always in the mood but never in the right mood. He came back from India with the obligatory dysentery and lived at home with his parents for a couple of years, doing nothing. He didn't actually do nothing. He saw every film the Three Stooges ever made, several times. He played squash, oscillating between the top two leagues. He took nice girls out to *Pizza Express*. He didn't smoke or drink or take E or smack, crack, coke or acid or go clubbing or have sex or eat kebabs or support Arsenal or do anything at all that might possibly have made him in any way unhealthy or impure or endangered or *fucking alive*.

Gabriel was a complete no-hoper.

Then he started modelling, to pay for his Three Stooges habit. (People had always told him he could, he *should*.) Then he met Christopher, who was dating the stylist at one of his shoots. Then he was invited to Christopher's New Year's Eve party and then he met Blanka. Then things started to happen.

PS.

Gabriel *isn't* Jewish, *can't* play the guitar for shit and *never* faints. Gabriel is a lying racist tone-deaf cunt.

○

Blanka was a very bad girl. She knew she was a very bad girl. She enjoyed being a very bad girl.

Blanka was born bad.

She smoked, drank, took E, smack, crack, coke, acid and anything else that was going, went clubbing, had sex and ate kebabs.

In fact the only thing that really screws people up that she didn't do was support Arsenal. (But if she'd known anything about football, she probably would've.)

Blanka's favourite colour was yellow, because, as she used to say, yellow is a happy colour.

She smoked seventeen Marlboro Lights a day, but was trying to give up, only it did help keep her weight down.

She'd spent the year before she met Gabriel (1994) staggering into various gossip columns under the leathered arm of the now-deceased guitarist of a soon-to-be-defunct indie rock band.

The year before, she'd dated the lead-singer.

1992 was the drummer. '91 the bassist.

She was widely blamed in the music press for causing the split.

People started calling her 'Yoko' to her face.

Somehow, though, despite the Kurt'n'Courtney life-style, she still managed to turn up for every show, shoot, lunch or launch looking as if she'd just been woken by a handsome prince. Nothing seemed to touch her.

### An Essay On Blanka

*As a beautiful woman, Blanka often desired some terrible fault which, when revealed, might stop men looking at her: an artificial limb to be unscrewed, or a false eye to take out and polish. Unfortunately, though, she was perfect — and the worst she could do was fart,*

*pick her nose or chew garlic; all of which had an under-*
*the-covers intimacy she disliked. Yes, her humanity and*
*her frailty would, by such means, be put on display, but*
*so would her coarseness and, by implication, her*
*accessibility. Perfection was protection. For a beautiful*
*woman, such as herself, even a fart was a come-on.*
*So, instead, she usually avoided going onto the street*
*and, when she did, she wore a headscarf and shades.*
*But beauty such as Blanka's is visible even when*
*hidden. Men still queued up behind her on the escalator.*
*She might wear a fur coat (fake, of course), full-length*
*and hooded, but her lines would still somehow be legible.*

All of which did not at all mean that Blanka wasn't
interested in men. She *had* to be dating someone. Preferably someone famous or someone who could be made
famous. Preferably someone with a good dealer.

When she met Gabriel, she was on the rebound. The
guitarist had dumped her just one final time: outside the
Hippodrome, in front of the paparazzi, as prearranged,
by their agents.

She had taken less than seven minutes to swingsway
through Chinatown and into Soho.

She was snogging Gabriel right there in the hall within two minutes of being introduced.

Gabriel was just her kind of man: tall, corruptible,
rich, hung.

As a child, Blanka had been spoilt almost as badly as
Gabriel. Her parents were Swiss.

Her upbringing was the best and most exclusive

Switzerland could afford. (She went to boarding school in Surrey.)

She'd been flirting with her father from the cradle on up, and all the usual girlish obsessions had been indulged: dolls, ponies, frocks, cars.

She had an agent by the age of 12, a modelling-contract by the age of 13, a film-contract by the age of 14 and a drink problem all the way along.

She was now 23. She had or had once had everything. What she didn't know about love and life and drugs was probably best avoided.

She'd met Christopher at one of one of her exes' video-shoots. (The band hadn't wanted dancers, but the record company insisted. Something to do with MTV.) She liked having a gay man to bitch with, to camp around with, to debate different styles of foreskin with, to empathize with.

She used to call Christopher whenever she'd spilt up with one of the band. Christopher would pad round the kitchen in his slippers, waving the cafetiere and sighing, 'Men.' (Christopher was more than well aware of the stereotype she wanted him to fulfil – but he could be real for the people he really loved.) As far as Blanka was aware, Christopher just did a nice sideline in cryable-on-shoulders.

Christopher never called Blanka. She just wasn't *there* for her friends like her friends were for her.

Blanka wasn't into that kind of emotional sharing shit.

Although Christopher always invited her to the New Year's Eve party, she'd never been before. There'd always been better offers. Gays weren't into coke and shit like that. Not compared with the band, anyway. More importantly, gays weren't really into *her*.

From the very first moment, she could be sure indifference wasn't going to be the problem with Gabriel.

She'd heard about unconditional, instant, everlasting love, but she'd never experienced –

○

*it*.

(Bom-*Bom*-Bom-*Bom*.)

It was like a force of nature. A wild abandoned passion. An overwhelming power.

It was all the slogans for all the perfumes Blanka had ever advertised all rolled into one.

It took place first in Blanka's car, then in Blanka's hall, in Blanka's kitchen, bathroom, rooftop garden, and, finally, bedroom.

Blanka had never known anything like it.

It was almost as good as crack.

It was much better than it'd been with any of the band.

Blanka and Gabriel took the phone off the hook and did nothing else for about two weeks.

It was a great time: smeggy sheets, daytime TV, chocolate.

Before Blanka knew it, Gabriel had moved in.

It immediately became clear that it hadn't been the right thing to do. It was the cause of endless arguments.

Gabriel would have to move back out again.

Gabriel knew it. Blanka knew it. But nobody said anything about it until it became completely unbearable.

At the end of the very first month, Blanka half-mentioned it.

Gabriel demanded to know what it was.

'It's – ' Blanka shrugged, waggled, flicked, 'it's *it*.'

'What's it?'

'*It* is!'

'But what is *it*, Blanka?'

'It's what it is, isn't it?'

'Oh, God,' said Gabriel, 'It's pointless. Listen – '

'*Exactly*. That's it exactly!'

' – it up to here with – '

'It's dead,' said Blanka. 'It'll never work.'

' – fucking tantrums. It will.'

'It *won't*.'

'What's wrong with – ?' asked Gabriel.

'*Everything's* wrong with it. This flat. This life.'

Gabriel approached Blanka. 'It isn't so bad, is – ?'

'It *is*.'

'Is it really?'

Blanka thought about it for a mo. 'Well, it's pretty bad.'

'Unbearable?'

'No – ' Blanka looked at Gabriel's feet.

'Intolerable?' Gabriel chucked Blanka's chin.

' – No.'

'Quite okay most of the time?'

'Well – '

'Then it can't be all that bad, can it?'

And that was where Gabriel and Blanka left it.

For a while, anyway.

○

'We met at Christopher's.' 'Christopher Goya, the choreographer.' 'On New Year's Eve.' 'Blanka was wear-ing this amazing silver dress.' '*Chanel.*' Young women walk from one end of the office to the other and back and back and back again. 'Long and tight and mmm,' says Gabriel. 'We just went straight for each other the moment we were in the same room together,' says Blanka. Young men carry pieces of paper, photographs, cups of coffee. 'We couldn't help ourselves,' says Gabriel. 'Our eyes met.' 'And then – ' The young women gossip about Gabriel and the young men make bets about Blanka. 'Oh, darling,' breathes Blanka. 'Yes?' says Gabriel. 'We made such a *fantastic* couple that evening, didn't we?' says Blanka, nuzzling. An older woman calls one of the younger women across from the other side of the office. 'Everyone said we looked as though we'd been dating for months and months before,' says Gabriel. 'We just fell into each other's arms,' says Blanka. There is a small queue of men at the coffee machine. 'We *actually* fell into Christopher Goya's bed,' says Gabriel. 'We spent the night,' says Blanka. Blanka is just about visible from the coffee machine. 'We went back to Blanka's flat, where we live now,' says Gabriel. 'For weeks and weeks we just shut ourselves away in perfect happiness,' gushes Blanka. 'We just stayed in bed,' says Gabriel. The air smells of air freshener, waste paper, circuit boards, coffee and salmon-and-cream-cheese bagels. We were such unbelievable slobs.' 'And we never had an angry word.' 'We knew we'd been made for each

other.' 'God, we were so happy.' 'We had so much in
common.' A young man looks over at Blanka while
holding a cup of coffee, while leaning against the coffee
machine. 'We both liked The Three Stooges – ' 'Chocolate,' chimes Blanka. The young man's tie tongues down
into the coffee cup. 'Daytime TV,' says Gabriel. 'Sex,'
says Blanka, smiling across at the young man. 'Of course,
sex,' says Gabriel. 'More sex,' says Blanka. The young
man has an erection. 'Lots more sex,' says Gabriel,
looking at Blanka. 'Sex and sex and sex,' says Blanka.
The young man goes to do some photocopying, coffee
dripping down onto his fly. 'What else?' asks Gabriel.
'Sex?' replies Blanka, turning to look for another young
man. 'Of course, darling.' 'The sex was unbelievable.'
'But then, well, we got a little careless – ' says Gabriel.
'What?' says Blanka, quickly. ' – and before we – '
'*Gabriel!*' snaps Blanka. ' – what was happening, we were
having a baby.' 'Hang on just a minute – "we"? Who
exactly is "we"?' asks Blanka. 'Well – ' says Gabriel,
looking over at a nice young woman. 'What's with this
"we"?' asks Blanka. The queue for the coffee machine
gets longer as other nice young women join on the end.
'Look, darling, couldn't we talk about this some other
time? Somewhere *un peu* less public.' 'Fine,' says Blanka.
A pause. The huzzing of the fluorescent tubes is just
audible beneath the snoring of computers and the
giggling of phones. 'And then, of course, when we lost
the baby, that just brought us closer together.' Gabriel
smiles at the first nice young woman. 'Darling, do we
*really* want to talk about that?' asks Blanka. The nice
young woman blushes and moves off, smiling. 'Well,

why on earth not?' says Gabriel, turning. 'Can we stop there?' Blanka asks the young woman with the notepad. 'Of course.' The young woman with the notepad has heard enough. 'Well, Blanka, Gabriel,' the young woman says, folding the notepad away, 'thanks for being so patient and helpful and, well, *nice* about all this.' Gabriel and Blanka and the young woman stand up and begin to walk through the office to the door. 'Um.' – heads turn – 'We hope to get the story out next month.' Walking. 'Our photographer will be along to the flat around ten tomorrow.' The door. 'Hope we haven't been *too* intrusive.' The corridor. 'Not at all.' The carpet here is grey as well. 'Any time.' Press for the lift. 'And, well, we hope that what we print will, well, set the record straight from here on in.' The lift. 'We hope so too.' Lift doors. 'Thanks again.' Closing. 'Bye.' Down. '"We"?' 45. 'Hey – ' 44. '"We" got pregnant.' 42. '"We" lost the baby.' 40. '"We've" had stitches instead of pubes for four weeks!' 37. 'Hey – ' 36. 'Gabriel, fuck off and die, alright? Just fuck right off and die.' 33. 32. 31. 30. 29.

○

At 12.00 noon today, following the announcement of the breaking-off of Gabriel and Blanka's much-rumoured and much-denied engagement, Connie Tripple, founder and chairperson of The Gabriel and Blanka Fan Club and Support Committee, issued the following statement at a poorly-attended press conference in the recreation-room:

*You* are to blame. All of you. You scum! You never allowed Gabriel and Blanka to be alone for one second.

You wanted to know every single little detail you could about Blanka's miscarriage.

You bought newspapers and magazines and wrote in to the letters pages and phoned in to the phone-ins.

You made the whole thing a hugely profitable enterprise.

You were merciless and insatiable and ugly and uncaring.

That was the *worst* thing: you really didn't care what you did to Gabriel or to Blanka.

You wanted information, details, trivia; headlines, front covers, gossip columns, cartoons; telephoto-photos, candid shots, topless pics; phone transcripts, angry faxes, wreath dedications; favourite colours, horoscopes, recipes.

Hoops, you made that poor couple jump through, hoops and hoops and hoops.

How would you lot like to be treated like that? How would *you* like the teensiest weensiest details of your lives to be known by everyone? How would *you* like the pressure and the stress of not ever being able to go out the front door without being followed, your every move documented, your every word printed? How would *you* like your pain to be turned into publicity and your grief into gossip.

But, no, you didn't think about that, did you?

You didn't think about what was proper and
decent.

You gossiped with each other. You nudged
and you nodded and you thought you *knew*.

But you were all wrong.

You didn't understand a single thing.

Gabriel and Blanka are far above you. You are
just a nasty scummy – eugh, something or other.
You consume lives, souls, babies. You devils! But
Gabriel and Blanka, Gabriel and Blanka are really
special people. Gabriel and Blanka are innocent
like little children, yes, like angels.

You never knew that. You never allowed
yourself to think about the terrible harm you
might be doing. You bastards!

You unfeeling, uncaring, unloving bastards.

○

Gabriel and Blanka lived together for exactly one year.

During that year they had their good times and their
bad times, their shit times and their hellish times.

But they did really love each other, at least in the
beginning.

There was something special about them, an aura of
youth and sex and happiness.

The first few months weren't quite as idyllic as they
sometimes liked to make out, but they were happier
than most people ever get to be.

They had their arguments, sure, but then they had
their reconciliations. Their reconciliations almost made

their arguments worthwhile. That was the equation that had to work out.

With Blanka's encouragement, Gabriel began to take acting classes. At Gabriel's request, Blanka got straight and laid down some demos.

They were really good for each other.

But then something started to go badly wrong between them.

Perhaps the miscarriage was to blame.

Gabriel accused Blanka of not wanting the baby.

Blanka said that was a lie. The baby was everything.

Gabriel said Blanka hadn't taken enough care.

They argued about this again and again.

The summer months went by: July and August and September. They were beautiful months in many ways, but weren't beautiful enough.

By October, both Gabriel and Blanka knew they were never going to be happy until they split up.

There were some legal things they had to sort out. Splitting up wasn't as simple as all that. They couldn't just go their separate ways. They needed a few months.

Gabriel moved out in late December.

They said goodbye for the last time on the phone on New Year's Eve, 1995.

They had both remembered the moment they met the year before and had both tried phoning each other at *exactly* the same time. They became desperate to speak to each other, desperate at the engaged tone. Eventually, Gabriel stopped trying to get through and Blanka got through.

They talked for a while and for a while they might almost have loved each other as much as they once did.

Then they said goodbye, put the phone down on their relationship and went to the parties they'd agreed to go to.

They saw each other, occasionally, after that, backstage at one of Gabriel's first nights or over other people's heads at one of Blanka's concerts, but they never spoke.

They were over, for each other, for ever.

# Postscript: Why Gabriel?

'I lived on the edge of all this indulgence,
Taking notes and trusting in prudence...'
– Lloyd Cole, *Speedboat*

Put it this way: I'm pretty sure I wouldn't have chosen myself out of a catalogue.

No – I'd've chosen something taller, slimmer, better-looking; something with 'good definition' – high cheek-bones, strong jawline; something with perfect teeth, deep green eyes, lots of black hair that didn't fall out; something, I think, intelligent-looking but still a bit 'rough', a bit 'untamed'.

(In other words, something a lot like Gabriel.)

Oh, and I'd've made damn sure I got a lifetime warranty on the eyes, the bowels, the penis and the feet. You just can't be too careful when it comes to choosing yourself; only the best will do when the best is going to be *you*.

It's what really matters, isn't it?: physical beauty, pop fame, planetary wealth.

All of this intellect stuff is fine as a consolation (which is how it developed in the first place: Socrates *not being* Alcibiades) but it doesn't make up for lacking the real modern stuff – the stuff that allows you to live in an up-to-the-minute world.

Not up-to-the-year, not up-to-the-day – I mean *now*, tomorrow and *whatever's after that.*

As far as true now–living goes, intellect is a real drawback. Because if you sit down and try to rationalize this world we're living in, baby, it's gone. Zoom! Gone even before your butt hits the seat.

You think, 'Hey, let's examine what all this shit over here might mean for all this other shit over there...'

You just *think about thinking*, and the world has already cloned and infected, videoed and morphed itself a billion more times.

Being dumb, as a whole generation has discovered, is the only really valid response, is the only true way of participating.

(Look, you're either spooked by the *Zeitgeist* or you're not.)

And participating is the big thing, isn't it? To be part of it all.

*Being dumb gives you the capacity; being beautiful gives you the opportunity.*

There *are* men that have all this, it's just you never see them.

You can buy them, sure – GQ, *Vogue*, *Playgirl* – and so they are 'available' in a kind of a way; but they aren't exactly out there, out there being men. Not in the mountain-bike-riding, sports-watch-checking, aftershave-wearing, bond-trading sense. You don't ever see them doing the business.

They don't go to art galleries or museums. They don't

attend football or rugby matches. They don't eat. Perhaps they have their hair and nails done, but the rest of us don't. Not really.

Where are they then?

Because, somewhere, *someone* must be living life as advertised. They *have* to be, or else take me out and shoot me *now*. If not, then why do the rest of us even bother to buy? Life as advertised, life as it *should* be, has to be available somewhere. *Maybe* it's a *rare* metal, *of course* it's an expensive and precious ore, but *please God*, don't let it be a *radioactive* element!

These people *do* exist. I *know* they do.

(Where are they then?)

They live in a parallel world of 'being beautiful and being photographed' – photographed because they are beautiful and beautiful because they are photographed.

Eventually they are photographed only because they've been photographed before, photographed by others (this has nothing to do with age; when they age, they vanish – abducted to tropical islands which governments don't allow to appear on the maps. Even governments worship beauty.).

Their bodies, faces, over the years, become graffitied-up, like toilet-walls, with each photographer, each piss-shit-wank-er, leaving another silly little message behind for the piss-shit-wank-ers, the photographers, who will follow.

And all the messages say, 'I woz 'ere,' and that is *all* the messages say.

I would have wanted this, though, for myself; I would have welcomed all the obscenities. ('Tattoo me with

# Late
# Capitalism

# Trains

When they first moved in they spent a lot of time not mentioning the trains: the trains that went by at the bottom of the garden. Their bedroom looked out, through some large French windows, onto the garden. The trains were about ten feet away. The frequency of their passing, as is usual with trains, varied according to the hours of the day and the requirements of the commuter. It was trains that, by their intensity, woke them up in the morning and trains, likewise, by their diffusion, that allowed them to go to sleep at night. There was a trick they soon learnt by which they could make sure that the swell and pass and lull of a late-night train did not bring them back from almost-sleep. The trick was to treat the rush and clack as surfers treat waves: either one let it lift one up and over, or one dove down deep underneath it. The mistake was trying to go through the face of the wave, the sound. They slept badly for the first few nights, but would not admit it. They became tired and argued about other things, but were each determined not to mention and not to blame the trains. Each considered themself to be coping with the trains better than the other one. Things improved, though. After a week or so, they started to notice only the trains which had gone by without their noticing them. They slept better. They made up. And a few days later, they noticed, rather strangely, that they were still noticing, now and again, the occasional train. It was only left for their first visitor to remark disconcertedly how remarkably quiet the trains were, for them to know that the home was truly their own.

# Launderama

i

I have always loved laundrettes. I have never not believed in ghosts. But I could have quite easily passed through a whole life, an eventful one, without ever having reason to bring these two minor facts together.

As a matter of fact, my life, up until the time I am about to relate, had not been particularly adventurous or remarkable. I had been abroad and I had come back. Whilst abroad, nothing unusual had happened. Any story I might have told – of drinking, poverty, mistranslation – my contemporaries would have been able to top. Most of them went off after university to teach English in newly liberated Eastern Europe, Prague being particularly popular. I followed the much more conservative route to Italy.

After coming back, I did several more uninteresting things before I eventually found myself, closing in on thirty, living in Ealing, in an old pre-Victorian house, across the street from the Launderama 'coin operated laundry and dry cleaning centre'. Despite being rather dull, or perhaps because of it, my English jobs have always paid quite well. (I author technical manuals and the occasional 'anonymous' erotic novel.) And so, although I was living opposite the Launderama, I had decided to buy – for the first time in my life – a washer-dryer.

White goods are another of my loves; and I spent a long time, last summer, going from shop to shop, enquiring as to the advantages of this model over that. Eventually, like the bourgeois I was rapidly becoming, I deferred to the Greater Wisdom of *Which* – buying one at least £200 more than I had any reason to. It was a Zanussi Jetsystem FJ 1093. The workmen delivered, but left me to fit it myself. This I did quite happily. Crouching, as I had to, half-crushed against the flaky skirting board, jeans picking up floor fluff by the kilo, I felt that I was getting to know my Zanussi, communing with it, earning its respect.

When I finally had it up and running, I spent two weeks doing my washing on an almost daily basis. I didn't feel too guilty about this, environment-wise, as the thing had a special programme for minutely-sized loads. To say I spent many happy hours watching the suds surge and the pants pirouette would be to commit self-parody – but probably wouldn't be as far from the truth as I might like you to think. I'm sure I sent the warranty off with indecently keen promptness. I'm sure I spent much longer than was healthy reading the manual. I'm sure I was far more house-proud of the interior of my Zanussi than I ever was of the inside of my toilet.

But the all-round improvement in my life that this particular purchase brought about had also one quite unforeseen side effect.

The house – of which the one-bedroom flat I was buying formed the first floor – stood, as I've said, diagonally opposite the Launderama; but, what's more, the room I had chosen for my study looked directly out across a medium-busy road toward this wonderful laundrette.

I haven't explained why I've always loved laundrettes, and perhaps I should. Most of all, it's the light inside them. This isn't true of all laundrettes, of course – and I do love them *all*, however dingy they might be – but my particular favourites are those dazzlingly fluorescent cubes that give you an artificial light-bath the moment you step inside. It almost feels unnecessary, after this, to put your clothes into a machine; surely such luminous purification has already removed all unwanted stains, vaporised any unpleasant odours and generally freshened your whole wardrobe?

After the light, I love the smell, the smells – that air-bath of stale cleanliness, the hygiene of other people, the odour of wool and acrylic and cotton and silk that have been made very wet and very dry within a short space of time.

There's also the smell of all the individual powders that people have used – dominated by the laundrette's own chosen cheapo brand (available to the forgetful in cupfuls from a 1950s style vending machine on the far wall), but modulated by everyone else's brand: sugary *Daz*, Aryan *Persil*, plasticy *Bold*, inscrutable *Cyclon*.

This is, I suppose, the smell of modern mothers and modern motherhood. As a man, entering a laundrette, I know that I am entering a still-female environment, a cave containing mini-caves, and that I must be on my best behaviour throughout.

Finally, there are the machines themselves: squat, slightly sullen washers, in dull metallic gold or blue, with chunky plastic buttons; huge, amicable dryers, lighter and more natural in colour than the washers (beige, perhaps, or olive, or cocoa brown), with magnets holding the doors shut.

All of this was what made me love laundrettes – but I think I loved them before I ever went inside one. (My parents always had a washing machine and a dryer.) I think I fell in love the first time we drove past one. (My parents brought me up in the country, far from laundrettes, far from London.) It was enough to see the clear-cut fluorescence – the obvious squares and dark circles that were the washers and dryers – the few, interesting people – it was enough.

I haven't mentioned the people, yet, because they become more important later on. A few of them, anyway. Though one of the customers I'll be describing is not of the commonest – or, at least, I think not.

To return to my Ealing flat, my front study – I had laid everything out just how I like it, with my desk directly under the window. This meant that, whenever my eyes came up from the paper, up from some tedious explanation or orgy, they naturally crossed the road and walked into the Launderama. It had no real competition. To its left was a shop selling bad pine furniture; to its right, the unit was closed, offering nothing more to look at than whitewashed windows and an estate agent's sign. A little further to the right, not really within my line of vision, were an Indian restaurant and a funeral director's. Off to the left were a newsagents and a junk shop. So, the only thing to distract me from the white cube – I remember it mostly at night, through the dark and often the wet – was the 65 bus on its way to Richmond. This would, occasionally, pause outside my window, giving its passengers a glimpse of a dark-haired man under an anglepoise lamp and presenting that dark-haired man with a menu of eight or ten explorable faces. But this did not happen often, and the faces were rarely very interesting. It was the Launderama that always met my abstraction.

The angle from which I observed it meant that the dryers were completely hidden from view, but the first three and a half washers were unobstructed. I could also see most of one of the two Formica benches that ran between the washers and dryers.

After buying my washer-dryer, as I said, there was an unexpected side-effect: because I no longer had any need of a laundrette, and because one was in my line of vision during most of the important hours of the day, I became almost cripplingly nostalgic for the whole washeteria world.

All the lovely things I have described – the light, the smells, the atmosphere – all of this had become past and useless.

I felt less that I had surpassed it (rising out of the world of renting and hiring and putting coins into slots and into the world of buying and hire purchasing and direct debit) than that *it* had abandoned *me*. I was a different kind of person – less public, less real; more decent, more like my parents. I was the kind of person who no longer used launderettes; and I liked myself less because of it.

It wasn't as if anything momentous had ever happened to me whilst doing my laundry. I had seen many attractive young women, arriving and departing, loading and unloading, washing and drying, over the laundrette years, but none of them had I ever seduced and few of them had I even spoken to. Which wasn't to say I hadn't always hoped. Romance among the smalls is a common enough fantasy for the urban bachelor, who meets no one outside his circle of inappropriate work fellows and unobtainable friends of friends.

I never took a book to the laundrette, always preferring to watch the washing and just be, just think – and much of what I thought about was meeting a beautiful young woman who had no washing machine at home, or whose washing machine was broken.

But I never did, and most of my relationships, as a result, were either with inappropriate work fellows (in my case, secretaries, publicity girls, desk editors) or unobtainable friends of friends. This made my relationships messy, short, unsatisfactory and painful.

The whole of the Zanussi summer, I was practically celibate – apart from a furious week's lovemaking with the woman who was in the seat next to mine on the flight to Prague. (My friends had finally persuaded me to go – and it was worth it, even apart from Sarah.) When we found, taxiing down the runway, that we'd both chosen the same novel to take with us as holiday reading (Kafka's *The Castle*) and, just before touchdown

– neither of us having read a word – that we were booked into the same hotel – when we found so many coincidences making up our romance for us, it wasn't hard to just capitulate to the mood of the city and the season. Our capitulation was total. The sex we had was almost as baroque as the churches we visited. Prayers and ejaculations, erections and spires. It turned out, though, that Sarah lived in Aberdeen (she was from Sussex), managing a choir. After we got back, we both agreed it would be ridiculous to try and carry on such a long-distance relationship. 'Unfortunately,' she said, 'you can't *really* fuck over the phone.' We exchanged addresses and numbers, and didn't write or call.

Looking longingly towards the bright world of which I was no longer an inhabitant, I still hoped that I might see the beautiful young washing-machineless woman, and I still pretended to myself that, on seeing her, I would have the cheek and charisma to rush out of my study and across the road, before her first spin cycle was even half-over, and charm and cheer her (she would be sad-looking) and, eventually, take her back to the warm, clean, newly washer–dryered sheets of my bed.

It is hardly surprising, then, that I stopped work immediately when, one September evening, whilst feeling, even for me, unusually incapable of concentration, I glanced across into the Launderama and saw a sad and beautiful young girl.

She was, as far as I could tell, around sixteen years old. Her figure was statuesque, and she had a roughly cut black moptop. Her skin, under the fluorescence, was doubly white. She turned, and I was able to see her face. It was elfin, slightly Japanese-looking, with darkly pencilled eyes and bright red lips.

If any woman had ever been 'the girl of my dreams', it was her. This – the beautiful girl in the laundrette – was a dream, albeit a daydream, that I had had for years.

And there she was, waiting for me, and here I was, staying.

Past experience, and past disappointment, led me to look for the man who would be with her – and past experience and disappointment were confirmed almost immediately. He stepped into sight from the back of the laundrette, where he'd either been getting change from the owner or buying powder from the vending machine. He then began transferring some dark-coloured clothing from his wash-bag into the second washing machine along. The girl was standing beside but slightly behind him, so close that they were obviously together. They didn't seem to be talking much. In fact, the harder I looked, the more the man seemed to be ignoring her.

The man had just started loading his washing into the machine when I saw the girl do something extraordinary. She pulled her black rollneck sweater off over her head and stuffed it into the machine along with his clothes. This, in itself, wasn't that unusual – what was was that I could clearly see she had nothing on underneath. For a moment, she turned towards the road, and I saw the small, very dark circles of her nipples. The man continued loading, ignoring her still. Perhaps it's a dare, I thought. Or perhaps she's trying to win their argument by this fantastic gesture. If so, it hadn't worked. The man had almost finished loading his washing. The girl now unzipped her dark skirt, at the side, and threw it into the machine. She was wearing thick black tights. She must still have been wearing shoes, for she next pulled some-thing off each foot and threw them together into the machine. The man was now reaching into the bottom of his bag for an elusive sock or pair of pants. Whilst he was doing this, the girl pushed her tights halfway down her thighs. She then sat down on the bench and rolled the tights completely off. I was now leaning forward, com-pletely ignoring the cup of coffee I'd made a few minutes before. This time, to my amazement, the girl didn't just throw the tights into the machine – she kept them in her hand whilst crouching down and fitting *herself* inside the washer.

Almost straight away, the man found the sock or whatever it was, threw it in after her and pushed shut the door.

I stood up and started to put some shoes on.

I might not have had the courage to cross the road to chat the girl up, but I had the decency to try to save her life. Whatever reason the man had for ignoring her, whatever terrible betrayal she'd been guilty of, whatever point she was trying to make by committing suicide, he had no reason to shut the door on her.

I put my shoes on without socks, trying to keep looking out the window the whole time. Helpless, I saw the man calmly pour out one then another half-cup of washing powder, tip them into the pre-wash and wash compartments, close the lid.

After one last look, I turned and ran down the stairs. The last I saw, the man was reaching for his pocket, about to produce the three 50p pieces.

I banged down the stairs, swinging round the banisters, rushed out of the front door, over the gravel and got ready to cross the road. Already, I could tell, I was too late. A number 65 bus went by, blocking me. When it had passed, I saw him insert the last coin and sit down. A moment later there was a gap in the traffic, and I made it across the road. The laundromat door was open.

I jumped down in front of the man's machine and tried peering in through the glass.

'Didn't you see her get in there?' I shouted. 'Why are you letting her do this?'

The man looked up from his book, a thriller. He was older than I'd expected. Far too old for her. He had grey hair. I wondered, for a moment, if the girl was his daughter.

'Oh, fuck,' said the man, turning to a woman at the far end. I glanced up at her. She was old as well. 'Another bloody weirdo. As if we need another bloody weirdo.'

'Get them to turn it off!' I shouted. 'She's in there! You know she's in there!'

'Did you see anyone?' said the man to the woman.

'There's only been you, so far as I've seen,' she said.

I was peering into the washing machine, unable to see anything. My shouts had brought the owner out from his back room. He was very familiar to me, by sight: a short, dark, Italian-looking man who always wore bowling shoes.

'You have a problem?' he asked.

'There's a girl in that machine,' I said, standing up and pointing. 'This man put her in there.'

The owner looked puzzled.

'Weirdo,' whispered the man, twizzling his finger round his ear.

'Do you mind if I check?' the owner asked.

'As long as I get that stuff washed,' the man said, after a pause. 'And get rid of him.'

The man walked up to the woman at the far end of the aisle.

'Quickly!' I said.

'Care in the bloody community...' I heard him say.

The owner went off to the back room.

'I feel sorry for them,' said the woman.

The washing machine was now churning determinedly, going into its first wash cycle.

'And call an ambulance!' I shouted. 'Does either of you know how to do mouth-to-mouth resuscitation?'

The owner came back with a bucket and some kind of override key.

Without fuss, he placed the bucket under the door, reached over the back of the machine, inserted the key and turned the whole thing off. The churning ceased and the amber light went dead. The owner reached down and sprang the door open. Soapy water flowed out, half-filling the bucket. Some of it slopped onto the lino. I dropped to my knees and thrust my hand into the hot, wet inside of the washing machine.

As you'll already have guessed, there was no girl inside.

## ii

Of course, as soon as I realized what a madman I'd seemed, I was embarrassed and apologetic. I offered to pay for the man's wash, and the woman's as well. I explained part of what I thought I'd seen. I made up some excuse about working too hard. I said I was a writer. The three of them just looked at me and waited together for me to leave. And, in the end, I did.

I crossed back over the road, let myself in, climbed the stairs, took my shoes off, sat down at the desk and began to laugh. My knees were wet. Then I realized, I wasn't laughing but crying. I might not have seen a girl murdered, but I'd seen one disappear. The fact that she seemed never to have existed didn't make her any less desireable, or any less missed once she'd gone.

As I sat at my desk, having turned the anglepoise off, I watched the aftermath of my explosion into the laundrette. I saw the owner, mopping some stray water off the floor. I saw the man and the woman, talking for a while, then moving apart. The woman finished her washing first. As she left, I saw her turn to the man and say something; he said something back, and she went off laughing.

After about fifteen minutes, the man stood up and opened the door of his machine. He pulled the clumps of damp mass into a washing basket and crossed with it to the dryers.

I had almost decided to close the curtains and stop watching when I saw a hand extend from the machine he had just left. Another hand followed it, pale but strong-wristed. On one of the fingers, I thought I could make out a ring. (My vision, at this point, is probably not to be trusted.) After the hands came a head, the girl's head, dark moptop, pale skin. As far as I could see, her hair didn't look wet at all. She pulled herself out of the machine, wheelbarrowing her hands over the floor. She stood up and paused for a moment, looking out of the window. I saw that she was still holding the pair of tights. Cars and pedestrians went past, and I saw they didn't see her. There was an expression of real pain and disappointment on her face — as if she had failed to do something she had wanted to do for a long time. For a moment, she looked up directly towards me. Her eyes were dark. I couldn't tell what colour, though I guessed brown. Her make-up had not run. She was exactly as she had been before. Then, she turned back to the machine, and pulled out a shoe. I watched as she slowly got dressed — tights first, next shoes, then skirt, then rollneck. When she was finished, she ran her hands through her hair a couple of times, stood up and walked out the door. Only, she didn't actually manage to make it out. She disappeared as she crossed the threshold. And that was when I knew she was a ghost.

### iii

There were a number of things I could have done now. I could have gone mad. I could have sought psychiatric help. I could have tracked down the old owner of the Launderama and found out the story of the ghost. I could have forgotten about it. I did none of these things.

For a month, I avoided sitting at my desk. Whenever I wrote, I worked at the kitchen table. I bought a laptop, and did all my typing in the kitchen. It was only my printing that had to be done in the study, and for that I kept the curtains closed.

I began to doubt the experience. Not to the extent of going over to the Launderama and asking if it had ever really happened. I knew it had.

One day, during the month, I saw the owner in the newsagents, buying a chocolate bar. From the way he looked at me, I knew it had happened.

But I was still curious to see whether it had happened just once or whether it would happen again, regularly.

I had only seen it once, and I had gazed into the clear interior light opposite any number of times. Perhaps it was a unique event.

So, I returned to my desk. Feeling rather brave and rather stupid about feeling rather brave.

Another month passed. It was getting close to Christmas. Often, even if the ghost-girl had appeared, I wouldn't, through the rain, have been able to see her.

But one evening, in the first week of December, when I was concentrating on my work and working better than for a long time, I glimpsed her as she was lifting the rollneck over her head. Everything was as before. It was a different man, though of a similar type – dull, beaten-looking, almost criminal – and he was using the same machine, the second along. The girl wore exactly the same clothes, and even her movements seemed repetitive.

Again, I watched her undress. Again, I saw her climb inside the machine. Again, as far as I could tell, no one else saw her.

But this second time, I did not rush across the road to save her. I knew that she would not be inside the machine when I got there. To do so would only embarrass another customer and further annoy the owner. I did put my shoes on, just in case I saw something different from last time. Just in case, when she walked out the laundrette door, she did actually manage to make it *out*.

I stood behind the desk, my hands on the chairback, watching the man as he stared at the machine, sitting on the bench.

And then I realized what I was waiting for: it was the moment, the less-than-instant, when the girl would look in my direction. I thought that, perhaps, if I could meet her yearning with my own, some form of communication might occur. I might, I thought, be able to help release her.

Something *was* different that night, though only a trivial thing. The man, when his load was done, just put it straight into his bag and left. He did not use the dryers. This meant that by the time the ghost-girl pulled herself out of the machine, the man had already left.

Even from my point of view, the laundrette now looked empty – and I somehow sensed it was.

I watched as her hands, then her whole body came out onto the floor. I watched her stand up. I watched her step to the window.

And, yes, for a moment, it *was* as if our gazes met. I couldn't be certain that she had been aware of me, of my intensity, but I similarly couldn't rid myself of the certainty that that intensity had, somehow, to make itself felt.

She turned away from the window and began to dress herself.

I did not see her leave – a 65 bus intervened.

That night I slept very well and did not dream.

### iv

I began to watch more regularly. I also began to feel as if watching wasn't enough – at least, not from this distance. I decided that I would abandon the still almost-new machine in my kitchen and do all my washing over the road – in the second machine along.

The first time I went in, the owner looked at me threateningly.

'Have you seen her again?' he said.

'Oh, that!' I said, as if I'd forgotten. 'Sorry, I was a bit pissed.' I wondered whether I should pretend to have been taking LSD. I wasn't sure if acid was socially acceptable to laundrette owners or not. I decided it probably wasn't.

'Pissed,' said the owner, and left it at that.

On my second and third visits, we did not speak, but he seemed to accept that I wasn't dangerous.

All this time, of course, I was hoping to see the girl. But I had sort of realized that she wouldn't appear until I became a more regular customer – became, once again, the kind of person that uses laundrettes.

This point must have been reached when, one

evening, I found it highly inconvenient to cross the road to do my washing. I had a deadline for the following morning, and, even though I could fax the piece over, I had hoped to get it done at a reasonable hour. The following evening, I was going on a date with Sarah. She was coming down to London for an interview with the Royal Opera. We had spoken on the phone, she calling me, for the first time in almost three months. I wanted to be vaguely human for our dinner – or at least as human as I can ever manage.

So when I hauled my laundry over the road, through the rain and traffic, into the Launderama, it was out of bloody-mindedness and a weird sort of lust. I wouldn't let the girl get away. I was convinced that if I didn't cross the road she was certain to appear.

The owner, for the first time, let me see his smile.

'Change?'

'No, I'm okay. Thank you.'

(Saving 50p pieces had become one of my small devotions.)

I stuffed my washing into the machine as quickly as possible. I'd brought a textbook to read while the cycle ran. I'd decided, as it seemed to make no difference, to do the drying at home. I was pissed off and in a hurry. I wished I had been able to let myself have the luxury of a home wash.

And so, perhaps because I was now, again, as I said, the right kind of person, I was just about to put my last sock into the machine when, to my right, I saw a black shape being lifted. I turned, and saw the girl, a couple of feet away, removing her rollneck.

This close up, with her back to me, I could see the nubs of her spine, the ridges of her ribs, a couple of moles and, half-caught in the down on the nape of her neck, a stray black hair.

She reached in front of me, chucking her rollneck into the machine.

I wanted to check the owner wasn't watching, but didn't dare look away in case the girl disappeared.

I put my last sock in the machine and, as I knew I must, started to get my change out.

The girl undressed just as before, taking no notice of me.

She was unbelievably beautiful. Perhaps a year or two older than I'd thought. Seventeen or eighteen. Her hair was naturally that black, as her armpit and pubic hair proved. When she took her shoes off, I saw they were chunky and old-fashioned. I began to wonder what period ghost she was. The eye make-up suggested early-to mid-sixties. A ghost that had been a fan of The Beatles – it was a strange thought.

I sat down on the bench, pretending to count my change. She would sit down beside me, I knew, when she came to roll down her tights. And she did – and I could feel both how close she was and how she really wasn't there at all. The presence was all of her personality – the density of her intelligence, the straightforwardness of her passion – but was none of her physicality. She disturbed no air, gave off no warmth, made no sound.

I watched as she, still grasping the rolled up tights, climbed head first into the machine. Then I closed the door behind her, put down my wallet and change, poured out my two half-cups of powder, fed in my three 50ps and sat back. I was trembling.

'I know you're in there,' I said to her, in my mind. 'I've seen you. You're so lovely.'

Forgetting my textbook, I sat, staring into the black of my jeans and T-shirts, the grey of the suds. Every so often, I thought I saw the side of a palm, pressing against the glass, or a ripple of hair, passing in front of one of the lighter-coloured fabrics.

'Why?' I asked, inside. 'Why are you doing this? Is it to die? Or are you trying to get clean?'

I felt like I was killing her after having already, the first time, failed to save her life. Yet I knew that, when I opened the door, out she would step, still alive, still dead, neither wet nor dry.

And so it happened. The wash cycle finished, the amber light went off, I opened the door and tumbled the heavy warm damp black clothes into a laundry basket. There was a moment, just as I was putting my hand inside the washer, when I became certain that it would encounter her soft dead white flesh. My desire, half for that to happen and half in terror of it, almost made me swoon.

I picked the basket up and crossed to the dryers. I had decided, after all, to dry my clothes there, in order to be able to watch her leave, up close. Hastily, I tipped the damp mass into the dryer and fumbled for my change. My wallet wasn't in my pocket. I remembered putting it on top of the washer. I turned, without thinking, and walked right through her.

I did not feel, as is often said, 'a terrible chill pass through me'. In fact, it was more like passing through a washing machine, as she had just, in theory, done. Inside her, where I for a brief second was, everything was hot and close and dense and churning. I was walking through a terrible emotion – an emotion that brought together jealousy, betrayal, guilt and fury, but excluded love. It was an emotion without explanation.

I stepped out the other side and fell against the washer, grabbing my wallet. I no longer cared if the owner saw me, stumbling round his laundrette. I felt as if I had just had terrifyingly intense sex with a complete stranger. I was gasping, sweating and crying.

When I looked back, after taking a moment to reconstruct myself, the girl had stepped to the window. She was giving her awful mournful look across the road, up at me, up at whatever the window meant to her. But, of course, I wasn't there. I was behind her. I wondered, briefly, if she felt my lack. After a moment, she began to dress herself.

I didn't dare try crossing the aisle, in case I failed to anticipate or remember her movements and again found myself within her.

I watched her remove her now familiar clothes from the washer and put them back on in the now familiar order.

The whole of this time, she was facing me. I could see an expression I hadn't been able to make out from my room. It was past mournfulness. It was a final despair.

More quickly than I remembered, she put on her clothes, her shoes, then left.

One last time, just before she passed into the threshold, I said to her, in my head, 'I've seen you. I've felt you. I can help you – release you.'

This time, I felt there was a strange acoustic to the words – as if they were going into something null, something dead. If this was how one heard hearing, I thought, she must have heard.

A minute or so after she had gone, I removed my washing from the dryer and took it back to my machine at home.

## v

When I unpacked my laundry from the bag, and was stuffing it into the washer-dryer, I felt something snag around my finger. When I pulled my hand out of the pile, I saw that a single black hair had wound itself around my ring finger. I placed it in my copy of *The Turn of the Screw*. It seemed the appropriate place.

## vi

The following evening, my dinner with Sarah went particularly well. We met in town and ate at the Coast. She was still high from her interview, pretty sure she'd got the job. She was also ecstatic at being in London, not Aberdeen.

By the time we got the bill, she had decided to forget the pretence of her hotel room and come back to my flat and sleep with me.

I had thought about the ghost-girl surprisingly little, all evening. Probably because I hadn't done much else all day.

But I couldn't help but remember her as we passed, on the other side of the road, the dark windows of the closed laundrette.

Try as I might, during the sex, I couldn't forget the girl. As soon as I closed my eyes, it was her that I was fucking. If I had known her name, I might have cried it out. As it was, Sarah thought my intensity was all for her.

### vii

Sarah heard the next week that she'd got the job. When she phoned with the news, I asked her if she'd like to try moving in with me. I wasn't particularly surprised when she agreed.

'That was love, wasn't it? — on Thursday,' she said. 'You can't fake that. I'll move in if you love me.'

And so I lied, and she moved in.

### viii

Despite this dishonest beginning, Sarah and I lived together very well. We rarely argued and always made up before going to sleep. Her job was challenging at first and rewarding afterward. She liked Ealing and even enjoyed the commute. I got to keep my study, though I worked — rather eccentrically, she thought — with the curtains closed, even in the freshness of spring. I was trying. I was really trying.

As it was approaching the anniversary of our first meeting on the plane, we decided to go back to Prague. We managed, after some explanation, to book the same seats on the same plane and the same room at the same hotel. But with our new found security in each other, the second holiday was even more delightful than the first. We both took our Kafka, and neither finished a chapter.

By the time we got back, I truly did love her and was quite prepared to forget the ghost-girl.

The flat, despite our happiness, was unavoidably cramped – so I suggested we look for somewhere bigger, somewhere Sarah could have her own study, somewhere we could invite friends.

Both our jobs were going well and so money, while obviously a consideration, wasn't a problem. We found the somewhere we'd been looking for, in Richmond, within a month. It was perfect. I could already see where my desk would go.

Because of the circumstances, it happened that we moved there before I'd managed to sell out of my Ealing flat. It had either been that or break the chain, and neither of us wanted to lose the new flat. This meant that, once or twice in a month, I had to cross the river and check that everything was alright with the flat. The estate agent had promised there would be no problem, but I had no peace of mind about its safety without us in it. I am a checker by nature and habit. I also enjoyed, I must admit, standing again in what had been my study, in front of where my desk used to be, looking through my old window toward the place in the laundrette where I thought I'd seen a ghost. This was the nearest I came to being unfaithful to Sarah.

## ix

The flat sold within six weeks.

I decided to pay it one last visit and to drop the keys through the letter box after I'd left. I was already a little nostalgic for bachelordom.

It was a summer Sunday. I wasn't going to take too long. Sarah was at home, doing a few things around the flat. We were going to spend the afternoon at Kew Gardens, which we'd both yet to see. Our new flat was a garden flat, which might explain our sudden interest in things green.

It wasn't till I was taking my one last look out of the study window that I noticed the change: the windows of the Launderama were neither bright with fluorescence nor dark with its absence. They were dull and white-washed. An estate agent's sign was placed in the window.

I locked up the flat and dropped the key in an envelope through the door, then walked over the gravel and crossed the road.

Peering through the laundrette window, in the oblong gap left round the sign, I could see that the washing and drying machines had all been pulled out. Pipes ran along the right-hand wall. At the back, the machine which sold powder stood propped up against a chair I had never seen before.

As I was curious, I walked along the street to the newsagents. Mrs Sumra was glad to see me again. I'd been a regular there, unshaven, for my Sundays. We talked for a while about Sarah and our new flat and the possibility of a baby, then I asked:

'The laundrette. How long has it been closed?'

'Oh, almost two weeks. It is a great shame. I know there are others, nearby. But it was the nicest one, wasn't it?'

'Yes.'

'But they only took the machines yesterday morning. I had hoped it would still be kept a laundrette by its new owners. But I saw them all leaving, lined up, on a lorry.'

Something about what Mrs Sumra had just said began to disconcert me.

'So it was closed for a fortnight before they took the machines?'

'Almost.'

I couldn't phrase the next question, so I bought a newspaper, said goodbye and left.

Driving across the river to Richmond, I realized that something had happened — something had gone astray. At the time, I put it down to my sadness at going back to a place I'd only just left and finding it already changed. But when I reached home, Sarah was standing in a corner of the kitchen, screaming, the door to the garden open, and a dead girl, naked, with a pair of black tights clutched in her hand, was lolling from the door of my still-warm washer-dryer.

The police said there was no way she could have got inside it unaided.

When I insisted on checking my copy of *The Turn of the Screw*, the ghost-girl's hair had vanished, but down the page in its place ran a long wet line.

# Flies I

It was on February 7th 1995 that the great breakthrough occurred. I had not been into the laboratory for several days. I was, in fact, seated in the breakfast room. I had woken early, unable to sleep. My dreams had been filled with an unpleasant buzzing. In one dream I was a dentist, about to extract a tooth; in another, an elephant waltzing in a circus ring. The final dream before waking was crucial, but does not concern. I showered, scaldingly. My usual breakfast: two twelve-minute eggs, three corner-to-corner-sliced slices of toast, a modicum of unsalted butter, Turkish coffee. It is important to have a strict routine. One remembers Einstein's suits. Such solutions are infrequent. To be scientific with one's life; the great difficulty. The papers contained little of interest and nothing about myself. I meditated for a half hour. My thoughts returned to the banks of the Rhine. A certain hotel and a Negro manservant. He was my chocolate golem. I think about him very often, though our liaison was brief, and wonder if he wasn't, perhaps, the love. The way his teeth were still visible, even in the dark. Their light source was sempiternal. If I were to meet him again, in a gentle-men's club or on a yacht, still, I would kneel down before him. Reassume my position. Worship is the only proper response. Discovering in myself a mood for the erotic, I polished my shoes. This was highly satisfactory. I am not definite enough about such things. As Mother suggested (was it really on her deathbed?), I should polish my shoes – at least those required *le matin* – each evening. If only Father had found such sanity and utility of utterance. 'It's gone into that hole!' I could never fathom. Perhaps he meant a mouse. Or a penis. He was not a man of much thought. My early contempt for him, even in long retrospect, faultless. His insistence upon country tweed, even in Kensington, in June. His deference to servants. (In public, I mean.) His jokes, which were not jokes but 'japes' or 'jests' or, *o mortificato*, 'jestlets'. I ramb. Breakfast disposed of, shoes spangling in the cupboard: Swedish exercises for fifteen minutes. (I am in danger of becoming Bernard Shaw. Must eat more veal.) Thought during about the calves of that Olympic slalom skier, last year in California. Bricks buried beneath the skin. I couldn't not touch. Luckily. The light through the drawing room window was exactly as required: unsentimental of hue, crisp of edge. I might have ordered it by the yard from Harrods. Positioned myself in a pleasant shaft, on the Bauhaus, to reread my Sc. Exp. Jou. Most dispiriting, this progresslessness of the past sennight. Losing it, perhaps. Gift. Discipline was required. To be eugenic with my own thoughts and discoveries. Weed out the Jewish; cultivate the Platonic. Pleased with this. It is *epimelesthai sautou* – care of the self. Good stuff. All distillation. 'Every day, in every way, I grow better and better,' in a more cultivated form. On the pleasure of this, descended to the basem.

How, one might ask, could the carcass of a dead dog
contribute to science? From curishness comes forth
sweetness? The damn thing was killed in the road
outside, last week. It belonged, I believe, to one of the
screaming children opposite, and its disappearance and
presumed demise did not encourage them to scream any
the less. Some ingrate indigent soul threw it over my
railings. (They still don't know.) I had meant, but could
not bring myself. It resides, even at this moment, on a
level with the basement window. Painted shut. Ladder.
Borrow. Aversion. Important work. Etc. Some day I
should employ some menial. Until then, since the
discovery, I am quite fond. I call it Apple, after
Newton's. Original name, I believe, from screamchild's
pre-walkies bellows: Muttley. Apple's decomposition
led to a notable rise in *Musca domestica*. Bluebottles. Her
maggotiness proved no intrusion, but her pupation did.
There is a ventilation grill. Grey and dust-fluffed. The
sweet smell of certain chemicals must have attracted
them. A general muscite decampment ensued. My own
downstairs Ethiopia. Intended to purchase sprays and
strips. Didn't. Instead, heroically, worked on. One day
only. After: driven upstairs, work impossible. Then, on
the 17th, yesterday, I remembered certain behavioural
characteristics. Reentering to the retort of discovery, I
saw again: *the flies are attracted to the lightbulb*. This was an
obvious. A difficult was that they were not attracted to
the *lightbulb*. Not itself anyway. How to describe the
moment. Though clichéd, Eureka! has the heritage. I
celebrated, as I have always done, since boyhood:
handstands up and down the stairs, face-slapping and a

wank. The flies were not attracted to the light, either. Why had no one seen? Why was I the first? Such intimacy of relation: flies and lightbulbs, flies and screens. *Flies and electricity!* The whole retrospect of their behaviour became dumbfoundingly obvious. Their obsession was almost worship. The bluebottles; their colour. An electric homage. The buzzing. How often in human history has the scientist mistaken a fly for a fizz, a fizz for a fly? And the fizz was a circuit, a fuse. It was electricity, singing. It was a *duo d'amor*. The fly is besotted with the electron. It is a suicidal passion. Those neon grids in the butchers: scintillating fly-sirens. Insectoflash. Light is irrelevant. I have conducted several experiments, in the dark. Last night. This afternoon, I will acquire several further carcasses for the purposes of maggot generation. Apple, though the darling of my research, is drying out. I will preserve her skeleton. Even her bark, my nightmare, comes back to me in fondness. I will publish!

# After Wagamama
# but Mostly Before

They laid themselves out on his futon, fully-undressed –
he on her left and she on his right.

'Let's just talk for a while,' the producer said.

'Why?' Nate asked, sitting up.

'Well, just because it sort of humanizes the whole
process,' the producer replied.

'Okay,' said Nate, lying back, 'what shall we talk about?'

'Well, before we start – I'd better know – what's your
worst-sex-habit?'

'My worst-sex-habit?'

'I mean, do you fart when you come? Do you stick
your tongue in her earwax and then straightaway in her
mouth? Can you only get it up if she's saying, "Fuck me,
Fonzie, fuck me!!!" – ? What?'

'What d'you mean by, *her*?'

'Her – Me – Her. Whoever. Tell me what to expect.'

Nate pretended to be thinking about whether or not
to confess. She knew he was faking qualms, but waited
for what she knew was coming.

'Well, my worst-sex-habit is probably I like to have
her give me a blow job while I listen to Yoko Ono on
my Walkman.' He was smiling, guilty and not-guilty.

'You made that up!!'

'No, I have it right here.' Nate pulled the Walkman

out from under a pile of comics beside the futon. 'Look,' he said, opening it up. A tape fell out onto the duvet. *Yoko Sex Tape*, was written in marker-pen on the label. 'But I wouldn't ask you to do that until at least the fifth time.'

'Call me a taxi,' she said, getting up off the futon and reaching for her T-shirt. 'Now!'

○

*complementing our nutritional philosophy of positive eating for positive living, wagamama has adopted the japanese management system of kaizen, which means continuous improvement*

*everyone concerned with wagamama is actively involved in suggesting and implementing small improvements to the operation*

*(from the wagamama opinnionaire, © 1995 wagamama)*

○

Earlier that evening, we went down to Wagamama to eat. There wasn't much of a queue. Nate ordered 23 and I had 26, like always. To drink, Nate had 603 and for a change I tried 1. It was all up to pretty much their usual standard. I like noodles and I like snooping on people, so I like Wagamama.

If you haven't been, you should. It's a new-style Japanese noodle bar. Fast food. Everyone sits on long benches, downstairs, in a not-quite-cramped white room. They fit you in just anywhere, so you and your partner usually end up sitting opposite each other between another two couples also sitting opposite each other. The waiter/waitress takes your order on a hand-held, which zaps it over to a station in the kitchen. This tells the chefs what to prepare. The food comes in about 7 minutes. It's like *Bladerunner* without the rain.

We were on the end of a table, so there was only one couple for me to snoop on. As – luckily – they were Loud People, snooping was easy. *She*, it soon became became clear, worked in Post-Production and *he* wrote some kind of literary gossip column.

I was sat next to her, Nate next to him.

As we sat down, she was talking:

' – you know, you can *over-style* something.'

'Definitely,' he said. He was gay. I could tell. Only gay men agree with women that quickly.

'Anyway, it's a year of changes.'

'I'm 26,' he said. 'It's getting serious.'

'Did you go to Chinese New Year?'

'I feel like I'm older.'

'It's the Year of the Rat, I think.'

'You mean *men*?' he said. '*You're* telling *me*.'

They giggled as their food arrived. Hers was 23. I was disappointed. From the way she was dressed, I'd expected her to go for something slightly less sad. She was wearing a baby-blue skinny-rib T-shirt with the slogan *Space Cadet* in silvery lettering, a silver glitter-look mini, limited edition Adidas trainers in orange and green, no socks; plus, she had a tattoo – the initials T/M intertwined – on her upper arm and a Kookaï bag between her feet with a copy of *Dazed and Confused* sticking out. (I've got a PhD in Fashion Victimology.)

As far as I'm concerned, ordering 23 at Wagamama is like buying a one-way-ticket to cliché-city and then settling down to raise a family.

I didn't recognize what *he* was having – perhaps something in the early-200s. (Like, spot the Alien From The Planet Sad.)

He was more laid-backly hip than her. He also wore Adidas, but with pale brown tartan trousers and a plaid shirt, untucked. He had a black bag full of what I assumed were trainspotty white labels.

'I know *exactly* what you mean,' said The Space Cadet. (I always give people nicknames.) 'I don't like Nina – she's turning into her mother. Australia! I mean, I'm-sorry-but-who-wants-to-go-to-Australia? They have no style there, no fashion.'

The Space Cadet wafted her Tic-Tac-orange finger-nails down her minimal curves, as if to say, '*Moi! Je suis la mode! Si je ne suis pas dans l'Australie, la mode aussi n'est pas la!*' (Subtitle: Me! I am Fashion. If I'm not in Australia, Fashion is not in Australia!)

I looked over and caught Early-200s trying not to laugh. By twirling my chopsticks, I got him to look up. Our eyes met. We interfaced. Our internal memo went something like this: *friends are people whose tackiness we can put up with (but only for limited periods); lovers are people whose tackiness includes having somebody – us – in love with them (for the foreseeable future).*

Early-200s looked back at The Space Cadet and covered himself by asking: 'Are you doing anything over Easter?'

'We're going to Oxfordshire – there's like nothing: no people, no nothing. We're going to take the bikes and go out into the fields. There's a river. Then we're coming back to London to get fucked.' The Space Cadet made a pill-swallowing gesture – hand cupped, neck exposed. 'You can have too much Nature, you know.'

'Definitely.'

○

*Hi, this is me and if you know me you know me and if you don't then you've got a wrong number but I'm not saying who I am either way because I don't want anyone who doesn't know me to know my name so but if you do know me and you want to leave me a message then the beep is coming up in about three two beep.*

Hi, this is Nathan. Look, can we make it seven thirty tonight instead of seven? I've got this film review piece to finish and my computer just crashed. The editor's really getting on my tits and I've got to get it done before the weekend and yeah. So I'm sorry I'm – I'll be at Wagamama around what did I say? – seven fifteen. Um – yeah. I'll probably see you in the queue, okay. Bye.

○

The evening before I took the producer out to Wagamama, I went to the NFT with Nina. They were showing Oshima's notoriously explicit *In the Realm of the Senses*. While we were having our tickets ripped, Nina asked me if I'd ever seen the film before. 'No,'

I said, 'but the producer says it's excellent.' Actually, it wasn't the kind of film the producer would've liked at all. (She mainly likes films starring Keanu Reeves.) So I was lying – I *had* seen it before; loads of times – in fact, I have it on video – but I'd always watched it on my own. Actually, I was interested to see the audience's – particularly the men in the audience's – interested in their reaction. I also wanted to see what Nina would say after. Half of me hoped she would say, 'Let's go to bed,' and the other half hoped she'd say, 'Let's go to a hotel.' What she actually said was, 'Do you have any condoms?' (I did.)

The audience, male *and* female, was actually pretty cool about the opening blow job – even the close-ups. I didn't hear anyone actually walk out. Or spew. Later on, to show how relaxed they were, everyone laughed too loud at the 'jokes'. They laughed at the scene where the tramp is lying asleep with his cock showing and the children come along and throw snowballs at it. They laughed a little in the scene where Sada stuffs an egg up her slit and then lays it, making chicken noises. They *really* laughed at the scene in the courtyard where Sada starts giving So-and-so a blow job in front of this old woman who's on her knees, picking leaves out of the gravel garden. So-and-so says to her, 'Hard work.' And the old woman looks up and says, 'Yes, but someone has to do it.'

The audience, as I say, right up to the end of the film, was pretty cool, pretty '90s, pretty *London* about the whole thing. But there was a collective oof! – from the men, mainly – when Sada cut off So-and-so's penis and

'When did you meet *Atom?*' he says.

'About three months ago,' I say.

'How?' he asks.

'*Sony,*' I say.

I suggest we go into the bar for a drink. Nate has a Sapporo and I have a vodka and orange. I explain to him how Atom is the most wonderful thing that ever happened to me and how, when we met, it was completely by accident: we were on a really packed tube-train, just coming in to Tottenham Court Road, when, without my seeing it, the headphone lead of my Walkman got caught up with the buttons of her jacket.

So, when Atom stepped off, I was dragged along after her.

We spent the first couple of minutes apologizing, then she asked what I'd been listening to.

'k.d. lang,' I said, which was a lie. k.d. was on the *other* side of the tape.

She smiled and said, 'Really?' and I said 'Yes,' and she said, 'Are you doing anything, now?' and I said, 'Nope.'

We went for coffee. We exchanged numbers. She called. We met. I called. We met. She called again. We met. I told her I loved her, and she told me she loved me, and that was that.

Atom, who is 26 and very ticklish, comes from Christchurch, New Zealand. She was over in London 'seeing the old place and the old folks'. (Her grandparents.) She couldn't afford to stay more than a month. Meeting me rather screwed things up for her. Sex had been on the travel itinerary, but not love.

'I could never live here,' she said. 'It's too dirty and too far from the sea. I'm sorry.' She thought that was it.

'I've always wanted to see New Zealand,' I lied, winning several International Prizes for Being Corny at the same time.

'Cool,' she said.

We kissed.

It's taken two and a half months for me to sort out visa and money stuff. Atom went back a couple of weeks ago to find a flat. I fly out in exactly twenty-three days, via Tokyo (so I can visit some friends).

'But did you always go for women?' Nate asks.

'Basically, yes,' I say.

'So I never had a chance?' he says.

'Of sex, absolutely not. I'd never sleep with a man.'

'I should get angry and call you a prick tease,' he said, 'but I like you too much for that.'

Nate's a sweetie, really –

○

*Dear Nina, just a postcard I'm afraid. I'm too busy looking for a lovenest to have time for the airmail stuff. I miss you honey. Only 26 days to go and I'm counting them all believe me. Put your fake pearls on babe and really think of me. I'm wearing my T-shirt. Love and hugs from your Space Cadet, Atom xxx*

○

Working in Wagamama isn't as bad as I'd thought it would be. They train you so you know what you're doing. The other staff are generally pretty okay and we don't let the customers (110 of them when we're full, which is always) hang round long enough to start dagging us. If there are ever any real trouble (and sometimes I wish there was), then the kitchen is full of sharp objects and psycho-chefs. But I won't be sorry to leave: I'm dying for home and I hate work.

Nina's friend, the producer, was in here the other evening. She was with some gay-looking music biz guy. (Nina had once taken me to a big party at the producer's. We'd been introduced and had talked for five minutes or so – mainly about Keanu Reeves' eyelashes. She didn't recognize me at Wagamama, though. Of course, I *am* the invisible waitress.) They were talking about Nina, so I tried to listen in. The producer was saying Nina was running off to Australia ('a shit-heap') with some guy called Nathan ('a complete shit'). I asked them three times if they were happy with their meals – and we're only meant to ask twice. (The producer was having 26, which is the one the chefs hate cooking most of all. 'But it's so boring,' they say, 'it's just noodles. Why don't they choose something from the early-200s?' '*Kaizen,*' I say to them, '*Kaizen.*')

Wagamama isn't the sort of place (and I've worked in a few) where the staff put spit in the food, but if it had been I'd have hocked one into the producer's 26. Bitchy cow.

What she said about Australia saved her from anything else I might have done – thrills ('She wants extra chilli in that one, please.') and spills ('Oh I *am* sorry.').

God, I'll bet Nina's just *miserable* to be leaving all this behind.

I remember asking her, early on, what she did for a job.

'I work in Post-Production,' she said.

'What does that involve?'

'It involves drinking a lot of coffee and trying *not* to smoke a lot of cigarettes.'

'So, it's hard work?'

Nina hates her job.

Speaking of Nina, I still haven't told her that I *deliberately* wrapped the lead of her headphones round the buttons on my coat *just* so I could get to talk to her and find out if, maybe, there was a *chance* she was a dyke. (I had a hunch, from the way she was standing – she wasn't standing *for* men, like most straight women do.) I suppose, one day, when we're old and wrinkled, living in some beach shack, I'll have to fess up. Then Nina'll have to stop making her cutesy little speeches about Fate bringing us together. It was Lust, sister – believe me. I was in a wild city. (Well, anything is wild compared to Auckland.) I was being wild.

The plan is, I go back and find us somewhere to live. But I also have to break it off with Marsha, which won't be easy after 3 years. She's always known it would happen. (She must've.)

○

*Wagamama. I like the food there. I really can't say any more. We had noodles. They were fine. Not too sticky, not too greasy. Shit. Shit. Shit. I should never have got into this business. Okay. Serious.*

*Wagamama's high reputation – or should that be wide.*
*Reputation of high-quality food, fast but not sloppy, served*
*at a low-cost to people sitting on benches. (Jesus!) Is upheld*
*in this my marvellous review. Oh God, you try doing this*
*shit when you're stoned.*

*As usual at Wagamama, you have to queue to get in. Next to*
*me in the queue were a couple, boy-boy, and the first guy told*
*the other guy the following story. He said it was true.*

*A straight friend of his, call him Mike, invites this girl, call*
*her Nancy, round for dinner. He decides to do sweet and sour*
*vegetables. He fries the onions till translucent, adds boiled*
*carrots, sweetcorn, peppers, loads of other stuff, adds ready-*
*made sweet and sour sauce. He washes the rice many many*
*times. Gets changed. Nancy arrives. He puts the rice on to*
*boil. They talk. They eat. They have Ben and Jerry's ice*
*cream for afters. They sit on the sofa. They start necking.*
*Then, suddenly, Nancy says she isn't ready for this. She'll*
*have to think about it. Mike is a bit embarrassed. They talk*
*and then she goes. The next morning she phones him at work.*
*'Come round after work,' she says. 'I've decided.' Mike goes*
*round after work. Nancy is there waiting. 'Okay,' she says.*
*'Let's do it. But I've got a special request. I like anal sex.*
*I want to do anal sex.' Mike hasn't done this before, but*
*he's cool about it. 'Is that what the problem was yesterday?'*
*he asks. 'Partly,' says Nancy. They go to bed and do it every*
*which way but loose. Unsafe as well. Mike catches the last*
*tube home. Next morning, Mike gets up to go for a piss and*
*finds a piece of sweetcorn under his foreskin. 'Wow,' he thinks,*
*'I hope she likes chilli.'*

*(First draft of Nathan Mifflin's review – unpublished – for the* Time Out Eating & Drinking Guide 1995. © *1995 Nathan Mifflin.)*

○

Marsha enjoyed her job, ticket-ripping at the NFT. She'd been there two years, working on her screenplay (*Tokyo Joe*) in the mornings.

She got to see a lot of great films, be around film-type people and hear all the film-world gossip. She even, occasionally, got to help look after a visiting luminary.

When the *Tarantino's Choice* season was on, guess who was there in hospitality, making sure the beers were icy and the popcorn fresh?

(Quentin was a complete sweetie, and thanked her personally. He also promised to read the treatment she gave him.)

Now and again, things got interesting during the screenings. Only a couple of days ago, there had been a real stand-up catfight between a couple of butchish dykes.

During the film, one of them started screaming, 'All men are rapists!' When she stopped, the other one said, quite clearly, 'Atom, they're not.' 'All of them are!' says the first one.

Then they started slapping each other round the face.

Marsha had to think fast. They were in the middle of Row H. She edged her way along the row behind them, broke them forcibly apart and said, 'Why don't we continue this interesting discussion *outside?*'

As Marsha escorted them out of the auditorium, there was a round of applause.

Once in the foyer, Marsha tried to calm them down – refusing to be drawn onto either side of the argument.

She managed so well that they both started insisting she go with them for a drink after the film finished.

Just then the film did end, and people started coming out, smirking at what they'd just seen and giving Atom and the producer (those were their names) foul looks.

'Come on,' said Atom, 'just one drink.'

'Yes,' said the producer, '*a* drink. Singular.'

Marsha politely declined:

'If I'm not home by twelve, my rapist gets worried.'

○

*The Sony Corporation started small. It was founded by a Mr Sony in 19–. Mr Sony himself was born to a poor Tokyo family. His mother worked seventeen hours a day in a Belgian laundry and his father played a great deal of golf. As a child, Mr Sony liked watching clouds form on the peak of Mount Fuji. He was a child with big dreams. His mother one day noticed him cupping his palms over his ears and making a Tssk-tssk sound. She shouted at him, 'Stop it, Mr Sony! It is very annoying.' This Mr Sony never forgot. The corporation began from small beans. Mr Sony began by selling —— and vacuum cleaners, door to door. It was a small neighbourhood, so he soon had to buy a bicycle. In 19–, Mr Sony set up his own business, Sony. By 19– the company had trebled in size. This was largely because of Mr Sony's hard work and his mother's packed lunches. Looking wisely ahead, Mr Sony*

*diversified into — and —. Eventually, Mr Sony decided to
retire so he could play more golf. He had a handicap of 26.
But before he left the company, he put his hands over his ears
and went 'Tssk tssk.' Nobody knew what he meant, until
somebody did. And that is how the Sony Walkman was
invented. Mr Sony is now the –th richest man in Japan.
He has a handicap of 23. He is a happy man.*

Excerpt from *A Child's History of the Sony
Corporation*, (Tokyo, 1995).

○

The producer and So-and-so are lying on their futon,
watching satellite TV. It is a programme about lacquer-
work. It is in German, which neither of them speak.

'Do you want this to watch?' asks So-and-so.

'Don't mind,' says the producer, who is also naked.

A picture comes up on the screen: Mount Fuji. Clouds
are forming on its summit.

'Have we got any more ice cream?' asks the producer.

'I think is now it finished, yes,' says So-and-so.

'Can you speak up, please,' the producer asks. 'Your
subtitles are fading.'

'Would you be like more sex?'

'Not really, no. I have to work tomorrow. I'm on the
early shift.'

A geisha slides through the bedroom door, on her
knees, pushing a tray. On the tray is a bottle of saké
and a couple of tubs of Ben and Jerry's *Chunky Monkey*.

The geisha pushes the tray to the end of the futon and then leaves, genuflecting.

'Do you like to working there?' So-and-so asks the producer.

'It's not too bad. If you like noodles and snooping.'

A column of sunlight caused by the gap down the middle, where the blinds didn't quite meet, has now reached the top left-hand corner of the screen.

The surface of the screen is grey-brown and almost-fluffy with dust.

After the shot of Mount Fuji, a shot of a quiet mountain village. The producer squints at the screen, which is getting harder and harder to see.

Old people are going about their dumb rural business – wearing triangular hats made out of straw. The camera closes in on a larger, longer building. It is a lacquery.

(Leaf-mist-hour.)

Cut to a happy-looking man, meticulously applying lacquer to an eggshell with a soft-bristled brush. Cut to a close-up of his hands. They are young-looking hands. This shot is held for about a minute.

The producer shifts across the futon, on her knees, and adjusts the angle of the TV. Through the gap in the curtains she sees Mount Fuji, clouds forming on its summit.

'The man my father is,' says So-and-so, yawning and farting.

'He looks well,' the producer says.

'Old film, very. He died ago.'

'Sorry.'

'I have here for you gift,' says So-and-so. 'My secret now gone is.'

From somewhere, So-and-so produces a small box covered in wrapping paper. The producer unwraps and opens it. The paper is stork-patterned. The box contains a lacquered egg.

There is a close-up of rain falling on bamboo leaves. Then a medium-shot of the lacquered egg in the producer's hands.

She brings it up to her face for a closer look, but as soon as she sees it on TV she watches that instead.

This shot (the lacquered egg with the producer's face, out-of-focus, behind it) is held as the titles run, rising like bubbles in a swimming pool.

The programme ends. A news programme begins.

'I don't care if it is your favourite film,' says the producer. 'No fucking way am I sticking that in my vagina!'

And she throws the lacquered egg, hard, at the TV.

The lacquered egg passes into the TV, hits the news-caster on the forehead, glances onto the floor but surprisingly does not smash.

A studio technician, Mike, discreetly picks it up from where it lies, spinning. It will make a nice present for Marsha.

'Watch it, So-and-so,' says the producer. 'You're bleeding on the covers again.'

'Quiet in the studio,' says a voice.

*Tokyo Joe: A Short Treatment*

*Set first in contemporary London, then Tokyo, this fast-paced
and very violent action movie (with a strong martial arts
element, plus a homage to John Woo) is the story of an angry
man's quest for justice.*

*So-and-so (Joe) is a member of a Triad gang in London.
One day, his best friend Keanu (Murasaki) is killed in front
of his eyes for nothing more than making a joke about the
legendary sexual prowess of the Triad leader. From that time
forth, So-and-so (Joe) begins to turn against the Triad.*

*Gradually, but not too gradually, he begins to see them
for the cruel oppressors they are. He stops them beating up
an old restaurant owner who can't pay the protection money
they demand. For this act of disobedience, So-and-so (Joe)
is exiled from the Triad.*

*So-and-so (Joe) goes into hiding with his loyal and
beautiful girlfriend Sada (Miko). They are relentlessly
pursued through London's docklands: car chases (sponsored
by Honda or Nissan), fight sequences.*

*Gradually, So-and-so (Joe) forms a plan. He must go to
Tokyo and challenge the Triad leader to mortal combat. It is
the only way. Sada (Miko) says she will go with him. They
have a night of tender passion, before they leave.*

*There are numerous close shaves on the journey to Japan
(fight-sequences, car-chases), but eventually they make it.*

*The evening of their arrival, Sada (Miko) is kidnapped
from their hotel room as So-and-so (Joe) takes a shower.
A message is spray-painted on the door. It is an address.
So-and-so (Joe), after getting dressed and tooled up, roars
off on his motorbike (sponsored).*

*The climactic scene takes place in a deserted warehouse.*
*Water drips from the roof and steel clangs. There is harsh*
*white lighting. (See* Bladerunner.) *The Triad hold Sada*
*(Miko) hostage, tied to a pillar, a knife to her throat — if So-*
*and-so (Joe) doesn't win, she dies.*

*The fight is long and hard and bloody, but eventually So-*
*and-so (Joe) bests the Triad leader — cutting his penis off.*
*(This part is optional, and could be cut.) The leader, because*
*he has been humiliated, begs to be killed. But So-and-so (Joe)*
*spares him, turning his back on hatred and revenge.*

*As he walks out, taking Sada (Miko) with him, through*
*the crowds of Triad men, none of them dare look at him. He*
*has won.*

*The End.*

*(© The Space Cadet, 1995)*

◯

Just before we went into production, the producer held a
huge getting-to-know each other party. The whole cast
was invited, from stars to extras. But, to confuse things as
much as possible, it was fancy-dress — and the producer
stated quite clearly in her invitations that no one — but
*no one* — would be admitted into her house who hadn't
made (and I quote): 'a serious and wholehearted effort
to come disguised as another member of the cast'. To
avoid duplications, a list was drawn up and names were
written beside names. Late responders were allotted
their identities by the producer. In a final attempt at
complete accuracy of impersonation, limousines were

hired to tour London, assembling groups or couples who would probably have arrived together in reality – whatever that is.

The party, like the whole production, was Japanese themed. The food (except for the finger food, canapés, nibbles and salads) was Japanese. The waitresses were geishas and the bouncers were sumo wrestlers. The ambience came care of a small Japanese folk ensemble. The producer wore a kimono-dress in electric blue. The guests, as they arrived, were given a small box wrapped in stork-patterned wrapping paper. The boxes contained two things: a black lacquered egg and a piece of card with the telephone number of a top gynaecologist on one side and the words, 'There will be a Surprise later', on the other. The invitations had been for nine, and it was now 9.23.

Outside, the paparazzi were fidgeting on their stepladders. The pubescents hoping to see Keanu Reeves clutched their stripey pink ballpoints and gazed up and down the avenue. The pubescents' mums stood in a broken circle, sharing tea from their thermoses and biscuits from their cake tins. The weather was fine.

Ben and Jerry (unrecognized) were the first to arrive, bringing a nice bottle of white wine and some hash cakes. Nathan's editor strolled in. Keanu Reeves arrived. The paparazzi went supernova. Keanu Reeves smiled, squinted, shrugged, signed a few autographs and strolled up the steps. Mr Sony, accompanying his mother and father, slipped in unnoticed. Yoko Ono and k.d. lang tumbled out of a limo and stumbled up the front steps. A load more extras arrived: Happy-Looking Man

(So-and-so's Father) accompanying Old Woman on her Knees and some more Old People From Quiet Mountain Village; Wagamama Chefs #1, #2, #23 and #26, Old Restaurant Owner, Atom's Grandparents; Irish Wolfhound, Martian, That Woman In America Who Got Away With Cutting Her Husband's Penis Off and German Newscaster; some Film Type People, the Boy-Boy Couple and the Couple of Butchish Dykes. J. Paul Getty Jr was about to be refused for being too scruffy, but the sumos let him pass when he barked 'Don't you know who I am?' loudly, in perfect Japanese. Mr Oshima, Mr John Woo and Mr Quentin Tarantino strolled up, deep in cinematic negotiation.

'The popcorn like just like *has* to be like fresh,' said Quentin Tarantino.

Then the stars arrived, all at once: Nathan and Atom, who were rumoured already to be having an affair; Marsha, Nina and Sada; last of all So-and-so, who nobody wanted to be seen with.

Mike and Nancy got a huge round of applause, both blushing.

Just after them Space Cadet and Early-200s ran in, late and apologizing. No one took any notice.

Everyone moved through into the living room, pairing and re-pairing off.

Mike was gushing all over Yoko Ono. 'I just love your solo work,' he said. 'Far more than your late husband's.' Mr Sony and Happy-Looking Man had already found each other out and were demonstrating putting techniques. Jerry, of Ben and Jerry, was getting quietly stoned with the Martian, who'd picked up some really powerful shit in the Horsehead Nebula. Ben, of Ben and Jerry, was consoling himself for his desertion by listening to k.d. lang sing Yoko Ono songs at the piano. The Space Cadet and Nate's Editor were already behind the sofa, necking. J. Paul Getty Jr was becoming very intimate with Early-200s and a large bottle of rice wine. So-and-so and Mr Oshima were out on the balcony, smoking and settling old scores.

Sada, Nina and Marsha were in the kitchen, helping the producer put the finishing touches to some salads. Sada was slicing courgettes while the others giggled.

'Oh shut up,' she said.

They heard a loud cheer, whooping and clapping from the other room.

'Ehhh!' said an American accent.

'Ah,' said the producer, wiping her hands on a dishcloth and rushing out, 'that'll be The Fonz.'

The girls carried on chopping. A few moments later she flopped back in, disconsolate.

'What is it?' asked Sada.

'He'd left by the time I got there,' said the producer. 'Buggered off somewhere to get stoned with the Martian.'

Down in the garden, all the geishas, whores, Triad gang members and rapists whom the producer had forgotten to invite, climbed over the back wall.

One of the geishas was wearing So-and-so's balls and penis as a necklace.

○

*In the preface to his early masterpiece,* The Order of Things (London, 1970), *Michel Foucault quotes a now-famous passage from a short story by Borges:* 'This book,' *Foucault writes,* 'first arose out of a passage in Borges, out of the laughter that shattered, as I read the passage, all the familiar landmarks of my thought – our thought, the thought that bears the stamp of our age and our geography – breaking up all the ordered surfaces and all the planes with which we are accustomed to tame the wild profusion of existing things, and continuing long afterward to disturb and threaten with collapse our age-old distinction between the Same and the Other. This passage quotes a "certain Chinese encyclopaedia" in which it is written that "animals are divided into: (a) belonging to the Emperor, (b) embalmed, (c) tame, (d) sucking pigs, (e) sirens, (f) fabulous, (g) stray dogs, (h) included in the present classification, (i) frenzied, (j) innumerable, (k) drawn with a fine camelhair brush, (l) et cetera, (m) having just broken the water pitcher, (n) that from a long way off look like flies." In the wonderment of this taxonomy, the thing we apprehend in one great leap,' writes Foucault, 'the thing that, by means of the fable, is demonstrated as the exotic charm of another system of thought, is the limitation of our own, the stark impossibility of thinking that.' According to the book* Japanese for Beginners (London, 1994), *the Japanese have completely different numerals (one, two, three, etc.) for counting different kinds of objects, namely (a) flat objects, (b) people, (c) cylindrical objects, (d) animals, (e) cupfuls, (f) yen. Michel Foucault never visited China, but did lecture in Japan on several occasions. This, however, as far as I know, was years after he had written* The Order of Things.

○

After everybody had eaten, and the sumo wrestlers had ejected the gatecrashers with only one minor fatality, the producer revealed what her Surprise was: A Karaoke Competition. Huge lists of available songs were passed round and people were asked to state which one they would most like to do. Then, as there wasn't time or patience for more than ten 'turns', lots were drawn. Michel Foucault, Borges and the Emperor arrived just in time to take part. The ten lucky or unlucky guests strolled up, one by one, to the microphone.

In the end, the running order was this:

1. The Emperor, *Instant Karma* (as performed by John Lennon)
2. Jerry, *Go Ask Alice* (The Jefferson Airplane)
3. The Fonz, *You Ain't Nothing But A Hound Dog* (Elvis Presley)
4. Irish Wolfhound, *When Irish Eyes Are Smiling* (Trad.)
5. Mr Sony, *(Get Up, I Feel Like Bein' A) Sex Machine* (James Brown)
6. Quentin Tarantino, *Turning Japanese* (The Vapors)
7. Wagamama Chef #23, *I Will Survive* (Gloria Gaynor)
8. Yoko Ono, *Moon of Alabama* (Brecht/Weill)
9. Atom, *My Girl* (Smokey Robinson and the Miracles)
10. Old Restaurant Owner, *My Way* (Frank Sinatra)

Victory went almost unanimously to Mr Sony. He was presented with a year's membership of the NFT. Atom and The Fonz were joint-second. They got an evening out, together, at Wagamama.

After the award ceremony was over, everyone insisted – clapping, cheering – that the producer do her 'turn'. But:

'Before I do my little number,' she began. ('26!' someone shouted. 'Ha-bloody-ha,' someone replied.) 'I'd just like to apologize for the fact that our budget didn't quite stretch to John Lennon, James Brown, Bertolt Brecht, etc.' ('Boo!' said everyone.) 'Some of these mega-megastars did hope to be here with us tonight – Elvis, particularly, was prepared to give his services free – but I'm afraid as our Martian friend will testify – ' She looked around unavailingly for the departed alien. ' – he had a long-standing engagement tonight at The Red Spot, Mars.' ('Hurray!' said everyone.) 'Also, God and Jesus sent a fax through a few minutes ago. I'll read it to you: "Sorry we can't make it, but we're with you in spirit."' (Everyone groaned.) 'And so, without further ado – '

11. The producer, *Somewhere Over the Rainbow* (Judy Garland)

○

*This is a work of fiction. Names, characters, places and incidents are the product of the author's imagination or are used fictitiously, and any resemblance to persons, living or dead, events or locales is entirely coincidental.*

○

At the end of the party, the producer called everyone together and announced that, as our new identities had been such a fabulous success, we should keep them throughout the remainder of the production. This we did.

# Flies II

It was the flies. It was the flies, you see, that first led me
to suspect that the man living in the end flat of my block
had murdered his mother. They hung about all last
summer. In front of the lift. There were, I will readily
admit, a few flies at the other end as well, but not half so
many. And then there were the grease spots on the floor
outside his flat. And the fact that the curtains were never
ever drawn. And the brown envelope, addressed to his
mother from the DHSS, which I received by mistake,
and which I posted through his door a few days later.
And the fact that the man had long dirty greasy hair,
black dirt thick under his nails, smoked roll-ups, smelt of
urine, went shopping in the Arndale Centre instead of
Putney or Wimbledon, was known to frequent the
library, was an obvious purchaser of pornographic
materials and did not have a job of any description. And
the fact that no one on the estate could ever remember
having seen his mother since the day, years and years ago,
when they moved in. He pees in the lift. I know he pees
in the lift. I have no evidence, but I know. I was in it
with him once, and he played with his flies. Itching to
get it out, just like he normally does. When I first
noticed the discrepancy in fly distribution, I decided to
conduct a census. As you will imagine, this was not

without its difficulties. I was not sure whether this sort of evidence is admissible in court. But whatever I can do to assist the course of justice, do it I will. I counted the flies once a day. Here are the results:

|            | My End:           | Murderer's End:     |
|------------|-------------------|---------------------|
| Monday     | 5                 | 7                   |
| Tuesday    | 4                 | 10                  |
| Wednesday  | 3                 | 5 or 6              |
| Thursday   | Rain: No flies.   | Rain: No flies.     |
| Friday     | 2                 | 2                   |
| Saturday   | 7                 | 6 or 7              |
| Sunday     | 9                 | Too many to count.  |

Conclusive proof, I think you'll find. Especially Tuesday. The police were not of the same opinion. I asked, at the very least, for them to apply for a search warrant. They called me a Nosy Neighbour Type. I did not take kindly to that. I threatened legal action, at which they laughed. Such disrespect for the law, even from its so-called guardians, is typical of the moral disrepair of our country. I stormed out of there with a cry of, 'Call yourself policemen!' Receiving no support from the constabulary, I resolved to pursue the prosecution myself. I bought myself a balaclava and a pair of binoculars. The man in the shop asked what I wanted them for, meaning birdwatching. I told him we had nothing but pigeons to watch from our flats, and all they do is fuck. 'No,' I said, 'I am engaged on an undercover surveillance operation. Top secret stuff.' He gave me the telephone number of some specialists. They rented out bugging equipment. They sent me some catalogues. I put them aside. But after watching unmoving curtains for a week, I thought a more technological approach was needed. They set me up with a kind of wireless gizmo. I don't know how they did it. I could hear everything. It cost about £500 plus VAT. All my suspicions were confirmed: he still talked to his mother. And he answered himself back in his mother's voice. It was eerie. It was like listening to *Psycho*. 'Would you like a cup of tea, Mum?' he would ask. 'Yes, luv, that would be lovely.' Sick. The things that guilt does to the human mind. I went to the police with the tapes. I was threatened with arrest. Cease and desist, that was their message. 'But he's got her body hanging up in the closet. I told you about the flies. You can't let him get away with this. He did it to claim her pension. Think of the taxpayer! Who pays you anyway?' I was arrested. Think of it. Me, after National Service. I practically got a medal. Never so much as a parking ticket. Except for the odd parking ticket. I was released when my sister paid bail. It wasn't very much. 'He's never been the same, since – ' she said to the policewoman. 'Since what?' I asked. 'Nothing, luv. Come along now.' They insisted I return the snooping equipment. I was served with some kind of order to stay away from the man. Then, one evening, so horrible I can hardly bear to describe it, he came round and knocked on my door. 'Mr Harris?' he said. 'I don't think we've met. My name is Jones. I live in the flat over there. The police tell me you think I've killed my mother.' I didn't react at all. He was as cunning as the devil. I tried to reach for one of my sticks in the umbrella stand.

'I thought we might clear this up privately. So why don't you just come round for tea. My mother's always wanted to meet you. She thinks your window boxes are so lovely.' 'Murderer!' I screamed. 'This is a decent house. Get out of it! Out! Now!' He backed away and I shut the door upon him. I phoned the police to ask them to come and protect me. 'Not you again,' they said. 'Please,' I said, 'take me into protective custody.' 'Why?' they said. 'He'll murder me just like he murdered his mother.' 'He's never murdered anybody, Mr Harris.' 'How do you know?' 'We just do.' 'If you don't protect me, I shall have to protect myself.' 'Mr Harris – ' I put the phone down, cutting them off. It was the first and last time I have ever done such a thing. The door is now fully barricaded. I have stocked up on tea, cake and evaporated milk. The bills are being paid by direct debit. He may try to starve me out, but I won't let him. I put my balaclava on and focus my binoculars. He doesn't make a move that I don't see. The phone is here ready. I have my trusty old catapult. It's a terrible thing, these people out on the loose. I blame the government and drugs and the police.

# (Untitled)

Sitting down beside me, the young man began with:

'Your name is – but, no, I'll keep that till later. I always say it too soon. You are 23. You were born on a Thursday in, um, September – between 1 and 2 in the afternoon. Your father says he was at home eating a steak-and-kidney pie; your mother contradicts him, saying it was chicken-and-mushroom.'

The train I had been meaning to take pulled into and out of Earls Court.

'That makes you – September – a Virgo: ambitious but realistic, calculating but tender. I'll work up to your exact birthdate. The 10th? I'm not sure. I have a bit of a blindspot for dates. Colours, I'm good at. And smells. At the moment you work in something to do with Information Technology, which I'm pretty sure is VoiceMail.'

When he spoke, his eyes were closed. He had blonde ringlets.

'Yes, it's VoiceMail. Every day, for lunch, you have a pack of Walker's crisps which you buy from the newspaper stall at the station, even though they cost 5p more there than at Sainsbury's – which is where you usually shop. Your favourite flavour is ... don't tell me, Smokey Bacon – though by the end of the week you'll often have Prawn Cocktail instead.'

Another train drew in and out. I didn't know why I wasn't getting on it.

'It's only when you get to the station on Monday morning – somewhere in south London – Wimbledon? – that you see the newspaper stall – Southfields! – and you remember that you always have crisps for lunch. The stall-holder is tall, black. He calls you darling, especially when you buy the Monday *Guardian* – which you get for the jobs section. You want to work in the media, if only in "a secretarial capacity".'

By now, I was late for work and ignoring the trains. There was absolutely no sense of danger.

'You've applied for about 20 such jobs, but have only succeeded in getting one interview. It was at a literary agents' near that cinema in Chelsea – what's it called? – God, I'm terrible with names. Anyway, the agent's name was Nick – no, Mick – and she wanted a secretary. You got along very well at the interview and she offered you the job. Unfortunately, she smoked 50-a-day and you couldn't breathe in that little office, so you said no. Where you work now is a non-smoking environment. You have a desk that's nowhere near a window and a computer that isn't as good as the one you'd like. There's a picture of Marlon Brando pinned up on the partition. (Marlon Brando in *The Wild One*, which is probably his best film.) Most of the time you are involved with admin. and low-level client services, though occasionally you get to make a presentation. You don't like being called a secretary. The company is medium-sized – about 100 people. There's a girl sits at the next desk, Madeleine, but everyone calls her Maddy – last week she was in Soho, out on a Friday night piss-up, when she saw this gorgeous guy standing beside a blue Mercedes. She doesn't know how it happened, but they ended up snogging and she spent the weekend at his flat. When you get in to work today, if you go, Maddy'll tell you all about how great it was. What she won't tell you, because she doesn't know, is that she has contracted the HIV virus and that she will die of a combination of AIDS-related illnesses in approximately 11 years time. Until then, she will keep her infection a secret. The guy she got off with, Charles, will kill himself in a couple of months time by taking some pills. I can give you the prescription if you want. I'm sorry – I didn't mean to make you cry – I don't really have that much control over what I say. I shouldn't've told you that about Maddy and Charles. Charles will leave behind a suicide note containing the names and telephone numbers of 13 young women. Only 12 of these numbers will work. The 13th number is for an estate agents' office above a nightclub in Balham called Skimpy's or Slinky's which burns to the ground in about 36 hours time. A cleaning lady dies, but no one else. Her son owns a pizza restaurant and her daughter is allergic to anchovies. Sorry. Maddy takes three sugars in her coffee, but is trying really hard to lose weight. She collects Pierrots, but would be really embarrassed if anyone found out. After the Christmas party last year, she went home with Jim – I mean, your boss – Mr Sanders. His wife had just left him, hours before, taking the kids and the Christmas tree. Mr Sanders bought the Christmas tree from a man at a roadside stall. The man at the roadside selling Christmas trees had raped 6 women in less than 2 years. He has yet to be caught. I just know these things. Mr Sanders has a birthmark on his back shaped exactly like a koala bear. In the early '70s he was in an R&B band called *The Whammie-Bars*. They put a single out on a subsidiary of WEA, 'I Don't Want to Know If You Don't Want to Tell Me (About It)'. It got to number 73 in the charts. You were born on the 11th of September 1972. The record at number 73 in the charts was 'I Don't Want to Know If You Don't Want to Tell Me (About It)' by *The Whammie-Bars*. Jim plays a tape of that record every day when he gets home from work. He really misses his wife and kids. That's why he's such a bastard to you and Maddy. When you were a kid, you were very frightened by the turkeys in the farm next door. You grew up in a small village, near the coast, in Cornwall. You once saw the ghost of a blind woman carrying a lantern. The ghost actually died in 1534 of the bubonic plague. Her name was Ellen Makepiece. She carries the lantern because she is looking for her eyes. At the age of 10, you moved to Guildford. Your father was a successful stockbroker and your mother worked for Marks & Spencer. They divorced on the day of the 1983 general election. Amicably, they said. But you heard what they screamed at each other that time in the kitchen. You stayed with your mother in the house in Guildford and saw your father at weekends. He took you to the zoo and to rugby matches until you told him, 'Dad, I'm a girl.' Then he took you shopping. You were a big fan of *Culture Club* and once saw Boy George getting out of one of the lifts in Harrods. You followed him out of the shop and down the street without ever daring to speak to him. He was very tall. You were thinking of Boy George when you had your first orgasm – which made you a bit worried you were a lesbian. (You aren't, though you once snogged a girl called Eileen.) You were lying on the floor in the bathroom in Guildford when you had your first orgasm. The mirror steamed up with the bath you were running. The carpet was green. Between the ages of 13 and 17, you went steady with Mark, who you still see sometimes. He works in the City now. 'A professional wanker,' as he says. When you split up for the last time, on that wet park bench, you went to the Chemists and bought 2 large bottles of extra-strength headache pills. The chemist wouldn't sell them to you at first, but then you told him you were moving to the Arab Emirates and wouldn't be able to get them out there. You had *very* bad periods, you said – which shut him up. You kept the pill bottles at the back of your knicker-drawer. Your mother found them and confronted you that evening. 'How could you be so selfish?' she said. You told her to stop spying on you. You told her to 'get a life'. A year later, you moved out – you moved in with Sarah. You got your current job two years ago. You didn't used to believe in God, but you've started to think that it must all mean something. You buy *Elle* and read it on the toilet, picking your nose and sticking bogeys on the faces of the thinnest models. When you look in the bathroom mirror, you wrinkle up your nose and stick out your tongue. Seven months ago, you had a one-night-stand with someone called Richard who you met in The Pitcher and Piano, Covent Garden. He was nice and the sex was good but he didn't seem that interested and you didn't swap phone numbers. You could locate his flat again, though, if you tried – near South Ken. tube – but you don't think he'd like that. You worry about growing older. Your breasts sliding, your forehead getting lines across it, your hair losing its shine and becoming brittle. You worry all the time. Every Wednesday evening you go swimming. But, Mary – your name is Mary – I've known it all along but I had to save it up – Mary, what I'm here to tell you in all this is that I *know*: I know *you*. I know you now and I've known you your whole life. When you were in the womb, I tickled your toes. When you were a baby, I chose your dreams. Through your whole life, I've helped out when I could. Everything you have done, I saw; everything you've thought, I experienced.'

There was a train in the station now. He stood up.

'Mary, listen to me: you are a totally lovable human being – from start to finish. And – er – I, I just thought someone ought to tell you.'

Before I could stop him, he jumped through the closing doors of the train.

'Bye,' he said, waving.

I took the day off work.

# Cosmetic

Though enabled by money, I was created by myself.
Even Max, my chief surgeon, will admit to that, won't
you, Max? What you see before you – man, woman,
child or beast – is *all* of my own choosing. I didn't even
look at the catalogues. They are skilled craftsmen, but they
have no imaginations. What limits them is the human
precedent. Anime and Manga mean nothing to them.
Disney was a holiday destination. At some point, before
money, dreams began; after money, dreams met their
easy enactment. Objections were made on the grounds
of 'nature' – is anything more ludicrous? What is nature?
Windows were pointed through: lawn, hedge, cows. A
brief lecture, to her, on the centuries of genetic manipu-
lation that led to the contemporary model of bovinity. I
revealed to Dr Schubert the intimacy of metal and grass:
no blade, no mower, no lawn. My point, and then my
money, was taken. Dr Schubert pleaded 'conscience'.
That, I realized, was the thing more ludicrous. 'Aquinas!'
I shouted after her. 'Jerome!' She did not look back.
Max produced the catalogues. I disposed of them and
produced Marvel and DC. Max took a walk beside the
lake. I think he was thinking about nature. I think that is
what is called conscience. I think he was trying not to
think about money. 'You want it, you got it!' His glasses

steamed up as he entered the room. A constant 45°C.
We celebrated with hot chocolate in the limo and vodka
in Geneva. I paid. Despite my unnatural objections, I
enjoyed the lawns. Cows, I despise, unless *à point*. Perhaps I should mention the mountains. Perhaps not. I
discovered a rather marvellous *savetier* and everything was
ready. Lights, absence, pain. Bandages, mirror, pleasure.
We had begun. I had my old nose mounted, after freeze-
drying. Restructuring, we had decided, though Max at
first had doubts (financial worries, I presume), would be
inhibitive. 'Begin afresh,' as my father said, after my first
custodial sentence. My mother did still exist, around
Opus 1. But after one too many sorry phone calls, I had
that matter taken care of. We even sued the car company. Opus 2: lights, absence, pain. Eyelids. An in-between
fact, but deserving. Opus 3 (I can give dates, if you wish:
8.31.99): l-a-p. I always wanted cheekbones, even back
in Boredom, US. Mangan cheekbones, with a slight
overhang (beetle or Beatle?). Max was having problems
with his wife. They had a daughter who found my file.
She was my first post-Op fan. Max found her a place, at
very short notice, in a Viennese boarding school. His
wife moved away to be closer to her. Long nights of
Max's bourbon and Max's tears. Opus 4: lips. Is there
any relation more intimate than man and surgeon? (To
this day the monster gets called Frankenstein and
Frankenstein is popularly considered a monster.) Lovers
we may, indeed, penetrate; but rarely do we alter them.
If so, only haphazardly. The wine bottle, smashed,
slashed. A club in Rio. Carnival. My chinos were ruined.
I would like, at some point, to call myself an absolutely

modern man. Opus 5: the new nose. Opus 6 (Xmas): a correction to the new nose. Opus 7 (Easter): chin and nose, again. Max's apologies became quite tiring. This time, my bourbon. His daughter had a boyfriend. Swaddled, I attended the Inauguration. The First Lady was ravishing. She thanked me personally for my endorsement. When I walked into the forests, alone, and followed the grass highways beneath the ski-lifts, I still picked up the winterlost coins. There were mountains. I tried to think of a use for the lake. My butler committed suicide quietly, without mess or a fuss. I therefore returned to the same agency for his replacement. I rate loyalty among the highest of the virtues. Opus 8: nose IV. Routine, though, this time. About 7 further on it, Max said. Perhaps 8. When one starts to keep a diary, one immediately becomes adolescent again. I maintained a secret correspondence with Max's daughter, 15. She was very fond of horses and cocaine. I tried to warn her off horses. Opus 9: nose V and cheeks II. I promised to marry her, when she grew up. This was not enough. I promised to relieve her of her virginity during the summer holidays. She seemed satisfied. June. July. There was a Goya retrospective in Prague. One of my companies bought out another of my companies without either of them realizing it. I think that might stand as a definition of wealth. Opus 10: lips II. This was not strictly necessary, but I thought it might provide an excuse not to kiss the prospective daughter. I kept my word, though. The nurse who interrupted us has, I believe, just opened her third beachfront bar in Malaysia. I am an absolutely modern man. Opus 12: nose VI. Golf. Opus

13: nose VII. Sometimes I lie awake at night and wish I could lie awake at night more often. There was talk of Madison Square Garden. 'Patience is a virtue,' as my father said (to the judge) after my fifth custodial sentence. Opus 14: nose VIII and ears. Why did I leave them so long? Dumbo. Max's daughter went back to Vienna for an abortion. She couldn't wait to tell her schoolmates. At least it put her off horses for a while. The first snows. Opus 15: nose. Between October and February: Opuses 16, 17 and 18. Mostly nasal. Completion could, at last, be discussed. Madison Square Garden were informed. Bruises permitting. The First Lady would be delighted. August. Opus 19. The finishing. Almost. *Coup de? De quoi? Théâtre*, of course. MSG. Monosodium glutamate. An artificial preservative. I am not 40. I am 20. Thoroughly modern me-me. Opus 20. Second thoughts on the nostrils. All the time I was on junk, I never got a cold. Taking Concorde is like taking bad cocaine. The foetus was on the cover of the *Enquirer*. It had my nose. My new nose. It was a girl. America: lights, absence, pain. New Year's Eve. Millennial. A different kind of theatre. 'I am one of the lost,' as they used to say, once. The metropolis that is my identity was jerry-built (indeed, my wet nurse was from Karlmarxstadt) about a central abandonment, a Nagasaki of the ego: there will always only be failure, within and about me both. You do not believe that, I hope. I never could stand the sound of laughter. The President will be assassinated. Geneva, Manhattan, Tokyo.

# When I Met Michel Foucault

*'I am no doubt not the only one*
*who writes in order to have no face.'*
— Michel Foucault,
*The Archaeology of Knowledge*

I

1. When I met Michel Foucault, the great French philosopher, he wasn't alive and I wasn't awake.

2. It was an August night, 1995.

3. Foucault died on June 25th 1984, of AIDS-related complications, in the Salpêtrière hospital, Paris.

4. I was lying on my usual left side of the bed and Vita, my partner of four years, was on the right.

1. It is not known when, exactly, nor from whom the great French philosopher, Michel Foucault, contracted the HIV virus.

2. When Foucault died, I was less than a month away from my seventeenth birthday.

3. As far as I know, I had never, in June 1984, heard of Foucault.

4. It was a clammy night and both Vita and I knew that the other was only pretending to be asleep.

### 2

The Foucault I met was the 1975 version. He was dressed in his trademark costume: black corduroy suit, white rollneck, oblong metal-framed spectacles, badge. His head, as always, was cleanly shaven. He was smiling his famous smile – the smile which has been described, elsewhere, as both 'dialectical' and 'carnivorous'.

### 3

*Since his death, Foucault has been the subject of three full-length biographies:*

1. *Didier Eribon,* Michel Foucault,
   *Paris: Flammarion, 1989.*
2. *James Miller,* The Passion of Michel Foucault,
   *New York: Simon & Schuster, 1993.*
3. *David Macey,* The Lives of Michel Foucault,
   *London: Hutchinson, 1993.*

*No doubt a fourth, of one sort or another, is already on its way.*

### 4

We had just been introduced by my Great Aunt Edith.

'Michael,' she had said. (Foucault had nodded, as if he knew her well.) 'This is my Great Nephew, Toby. He is 28. He is a great fan – if that is the word – of your work.'

Great Aunt Edith had then laughed her characteristic laugh – a sort of half-drowned glottal cooing.

'It is a pleasure,' Foucault had said.

'It isn't the word,' I said.

## 5

*Of the three biographies of Foucault, Didier Eribon's came first. Originally published in French (1989) before being translated into English (1992), this is an essential source of basic information about Foucault.*

*However, Eribon's is far too coy on at least four crucial issues: Foucault's homosexuality, his involvement in extreme sado-masochistic practices, his contraction of the HIV virus and his decision to keep the nature of his final illness secret.*

*This, I suspect, is the expression of Eribon's implicit desire to preserve intact his already established image of Foucault.*

*Eribon's greatest strength is his insider's knowledge of the machinations and patronages of the French educational system at its highest levels. This is a non-academic biography of Foucault, Foucault the academic — not Foucault the homosexual, the friend, the person, the soul.*

*Although good on the controversies (for instance, that of Spring 1968 with Jean-Paul Sartre), Eribon is very poor on the texts themselves.*

*He is the only one of the three biographers to have known Foucault.*

## 6

Introductions completed, my Great Aunt Edith walked across to the Bechstein Grand which used to stand in front of the French windows in what was her sitting room.

It was 1975 or 1976 that this visit happened.

I am seven or eight. I am visiting with my parents.

I am sitting on something soft and chintzy, listening to my Great Aunt Edith as she begins to tinkle out some of her favourite Debussy – music which, in life, in my lifetime, she was always too arthritic to manage.

She is smiling, which makes me feel happy, even though her playing is not all that good.

I watch as, like chintz, she fades.

7

*The two other biographies of Foucault came out at almost exactly the same moment, and were several times reviewed side by side. To take them one at a time:*

*Though undoubtedly overdependent upon Eribon's earlier biography, particularly in the early chapters, David Macey's* The Lives of Michel Foucault *is a competent if rarely inspired attempt.*

*His own original research has turned up one or two interesting minor facts about Foucault:*

*1. That, as a child, Foucault had a strong desire to be a goldfish (p. 14).*
*2. That Foucault always helped with the family gherkin harvest (p. 19).*
*3. That Foucault once elaborated a whole theory about his particular culinary speciality, pasta (p. 74).*
*4. That Foucault and the great French structuralist, Roland Barthes, were occasional lovers (p. 82).*
*1. That Foucault was friends with the English actress Julie Christie – for whom he carefully prepared vegetarian meals (p. 239).*

*2. That Foucault couldn't tell the difference between
David Bowie and Mick Jagger (p. 399).
3. That Foucault and Roland Barthes both died in the
Salpêtrière Hospital, Paris (p. 428).
4. That Foucault once wet himself with excitement, whilst
travelling to martial law Poland (p. 447).*

*But though basically well-written, the book feels less like a
biography than a rehearsal for a biography.*

*Macey, to give him his due, is stronger than Eribon on
Foucault's texts, major and minor. Yet each text, though neatly
summarised, is never intellectually engaged with.*

The Lives of Michel Foucault *passes completely unmen-
tioned in the index and bibliography of* The Cambridge
Companion to Foucault, *(New York: Cambridge University Press, 1994). This omission, if it occurred by accident,
confirms the negligible standing of this book among Foucault
scholars; if by design, merely redoubles that confirmation.*

*One may safely use this biography as a footrest, while one
enjoys the other two.*

## 8

We were in a San Francisco bar. There were extravagant
hubcaps and colourful baseball pennants on the wall,
along with posters of the early Elvis Presley and the late
James Dean. Music soared out from a neon cathedral
of a jukebox: no groups but girl-groups, no producer
but Phil Spector – The Ronettes, The Crystals, Darlene
Love and others. There was something inexorably
shoddy about the whole deliberate effect. It made me

feel a faint nostalgia for the late Fifties and early Sixties (I was born in 1968) – a nostalgia warm and flat as bottom-of-the-can Pepsi.

I launched myself onto the unusually tall high-stool beside Foucault's.

'That's cool,' said Foucault, pointing to something on my chest.

I looked down and saw I was wearing a badge – what, in America, they call a 'button'. The badge was blue with white lettering. The slogan on the badge read:

'How do you like my badge?' Foucault asked, lifting his black lapel up to my face.

His badge was black with white lettering. Its slogan read:

'Cool,' I said.

'Would you like a drink, Toby?' Foucault asked.

## 9

*Of the three biographies of Foucault, James Miller's* The
Passion of Michel Foucault *is by far the best. His investigation of Foucault's sexuality (the 'passion' of the title) is detailed
and considered, though some have accused him of distortion and
homophobia.*

*Miller himself reads Foucault's texts with a 'passion'. Some-
thing, we feel, is really at stake here – something more than
delivering a decent academic biography.*

*While obviously indebted to Eribon, as all future biographers
will inevitably be, Miller is never enslaved by prior research.*

*His interpretation of Foucault's work, heavily dependent on
their author's fascination with 'limit-experiences', is a very
powerful one – with all the faults of overemphasis that entails.*

*If you are only ever going to read one Foucault biography,
make it this one.*

## 10

Use of my first name in this way, at the end of a sentence,
always makes me nervous. The fact that Foucault's smile
was at this moment definitely more carnivorous than
dialectical, made me even more jittery.

'Sure,' I said, in my best attempted–Californian (which
came out sounding more like failed–Brooklyn).

'What?' he asked, a little too fast. '*What* will you
have?'

This was a test – I could tell. This was a mini-*agrégation*. He was looking at me as if I were a text, a victim, a student, a soul.

The pale blue of his eyes was prinked with sexual intelligence, sexual wit.

'Coors?' I said, hopefully.

'A Coors,' Foucault said to the barman, 'and a Bud.'

'Shit!' I said, knowing I had failed.

'Don't worry,' Foucault said. 'You can always retake. That's what I did.'

The drinks arrived. Foucault told the barman to put it on the tab. From under the bar, the barman – who bore some resemblance to the great German philosopher, Friedrich Nietzsche – brought out a pink baseball bat.

'Pay,' he said.

Foucault paid.

I looked round the bar and took a slug of my Coors. It tasted of The British Library. The bar was empty for the time of day (early afternoon).

I was wearing mostly my usual: black Gap poloneck, brown Gap jeans, black DMs, round specs.

The badge was an unexpected addition.

## I I

*Vita shifted her position to indicate that she wasn't really asleep and to discover if I was.*

*I pretended to be beautifully unconscious.*

*Vita got up to get a glass of water.*

*In my half-sleep, certain questions occurred:*

*1. How did Great Aunt Edith know Foucault?*

*2. Was Great Aunt Edith really, after all, French, as she, in her final delirium, had claimed?*

*3. Wasn't it Ravel and not Debussy that had been her favourite composer?*

*4. And hadn't our visit been a lot later?*

*1. In 1983 or 1984?*

*2. And wasn't a professional pianist, an embarrassed young man in tails, engaged for our pleasure, for Great Aunt Edith's pleasure, for the afternoon, for £50?*

*3. Didn't Great Aunt Edith call me aside and say 'We'll settle up now, then'?*

*4. And didn't I have to find some polite way of saying, 'I'm sorry, Great Aunt Edith, but I'm not the person you think I am'?*

12

'Shall we have a conversation?' Foucault asked, very politely.

I looked at his badge. It had changed colour from white (lettering) on black (background) to pink on white. Its slogan now read:

CULTIVATE YOUR
LEGITIMATE
STRANGENESS

I looked at my badge. Its colours had reversed — from white on blue to blue on white. Its slogan had changed, becoming:

'Toby?' Foucault inquired.

'It's a great honour to meet you, sir.'

Foucault took a large swig of Bud then looked at me, dialectically.

'How's your beer?' he asked.


## 13

*I heard a tinkle. There was a possibility that it was one of four things:*

- *Vita peeing in the bathroom*
- *Great Aunt Edith playing Debussy*
- *Friedrich Nietzsche, the great German barman,*
  *pouring out a measure of liquor*
- *the word 'tinkle'*

*I dismissed the final possibility as too silly.*

14

'It tastes of The British Library,' I said.

'Which part?' Foucault shouted, suddenly electrified (I expect because I had mentioned one of his great passions: archives). Barman-Nietzsche looked up, moustache abristle.

'The Main Reading Room, of course.'

'Which seat?'

'D16.'

There was a pause as Foucault took this information in. The wrinkles moved up and down his cranial dome, like intellectual tides. I got the feeling I had given the right answer. Barman-Nietzsche looked down again. I ventured a question.

'Why, what does yours taste like?'

'Mine tastes like Nefertiti.'

'Sounds a bit dry,' I said.

'Shall we go somewhere else?' Foucault asked, finishing his Bud.

'Where would you like to go, Mr Foucault?' I asked.

'Call me Michel, or Michael, or just Mike,' said Foucault.

'I don't think I can call you Mike – you're not a Mike-type.'

'Mike like 'mike' like 'microphone'. Or Mick like Jagger. Or Mickey like Mouse. Call me Mickey.'

'Please, can't I just call you Michel?'

'Finish your Coors,' said Foucault. 'We're leaving.'

15

*The toilet flushed and the taps began to run. The taps went off and then the lights. The bedroom door opened. Closed. The bed made no sound as Vita got in and shifted over to my side. I sneaked a look at the luminous face of my alarm clock: 2.15. Then 2.16.*

16

I finished my Coors.

We left the bar.

We walked across the parking lot to Foucault's silver, white, pink and red Thunderbird convertible. The heat coming up off the tarmac was like a twin, a doppel-gänger, a ghost, a soul.

We powered up the coastal road and into San Francisco, Foucault wearing driving goggles.

As we crossed the Golden Gate Bridge, the Pacific sunset to our right looked like something an acid-frazzled hippy would spraypaint on the back of their crombie.

17

*'Are you awake?' Vita asked.*

18

When we arrived at his apartment block, Foucault tossed the driving-goggles onto the white leather of the back seat.

'Won't somebody steal them?' I asked.

'It's a very safe area; there's no need to be worried.'
Foucault put his spectacles back on.

19

*'You're awake, aren't you?'*

20

'This is where I live,' said Foucault, as we mounted the
spiral staircase to the eighth floor. '285 rue de Vaugirard,
Paris XVe.'

As I looked down – climbing, turning – I remembered a hundred murderous film-sequences: Buñuel,
Hitchcock, Polanski, Spielberg.

In the far distance, I could almost hear the sirens,
police and ambulance, Homeric and Joycean, of my own
violent and approaching death.

Foucault put his hand firmly on my shoulder.

I tensed up, ready to be hefted over the smooth banisters. I prepared my body for the false flight of the fall. I
anticipated landing, in a smash of sweat, in a scream of
spiders, beside a startled, woken Vita.

I was more afraid of this being only another boring
falling-dream than of this not being a dream at all.

'Come on, Toby,' said Foucault. 'We don't want to
miss the start.'

Foucault's apartment was on the top floor.

As we stood before the door, Foucault turned toward
me and, in an unnecessarily conspiratorial tone,

whispered: 'We are no longer in France. We are now in Sidi Bou Saïd. I keep a secret apartment here. It is in Sidi Bou Saïd that I first shaved my head.'

'And wrote *The Archaeology of Knowledge*.'

'Shaving my head was, perhaps, the more significant of the two acts,' said Foucault, turning the key and opening the door.

21

*The subconscious (Foucault would undoubtedly disagree here) is the realm of the utterly tedious.*

*I am going to have a badge made, red with green lettering:*

*Foucault's (green on pink) counterbadge would read:*

*If I dream at all, I usually dream about The Bee Gees (circa 1977): Maurice Gibb, mostly — but sometimes Barry. Never, for some reason, 'the other one'.*

*(I once saw Maurice — in the flesh, in Blackwells, in Oxford, in the Philosophy Section. He looked lost so I asked him what he was looking for. 'Cookery,' he said. I gave him directions to the Travel section and hid behind Psychoanalysis in case he came back. He didn't.)*

*I doubt that Freud has much to say about The Bee Gees. I doubt that Maurice, Barry or even 'the other one' much pre-occupy Jung or Klein or Lacan.*

*(This is why I was so pleased to have exchanged dreams of a cheesy US pop group, if only temporarily, for dreams of a great French philosopher.)*

## 22

The first thing I noticed as we entered the flat was how cool and quiet it was.

'You wait in my study,' Foucault ordered. 'I will just change my clothes.'

Foucault's black corduroys *did* look a little hot for California, or Tunisia, so I quite understood his wanting to change.

I walked through a high archway into Foucault's study. One wall was covered with books and periodicals; the other three were whitewashed and unadorned. A great light, coming from a tall window in the far wall, suffused the room.

The view from the window was of square white rooftops patterned with geometrical shadows, of white linen on long washing-lines, of blue sky and of more blue sky.

My attention was immediately drawn to Foucault's desk. It was here that the light was most intense.

Apart from the neat stacks of paper, the typewriter, the writing implements and the copy of *Le Monde*, there were two remarkable objects resting upon it.

### 23

'Toby?'

### 24

One was a human skull.

As it was still pale white, and had not aged to a dark yellow, I assumed it was the skull of someone not yet four years dead.

I tipped the cranium backward with my palm and inspected the teeth: there were four fillings, arranged symmetrically.

For a moment I thought I heard Foucault coming, so I cracked the jaws back together and jumped to the window. When, after a minute, he still had not appeared, I returned to the desk.

The skull was acting as a paperweight. I lifted it up and tried to read the title page lying beneath it, but was unable to: it was in Arab script.

I hurriedly turned a few pages over to try to find some French or English or Latin, but it was all equally indecipherable.

Finally, about twenty pages in, I found an ink drawing of two men, each with the other's penis in their mouth. One of the men had a cleanly shaven head and was wearing oblong metal-framed spectacles.

I replaced the skull and turned my attention to the second object of fascination.

### 25

*Michel Foucault was, in my humble opinion, one of the weirdest emanations our planet and species has ever put forth. His was an orchidaceous intellect: poisonous and succulent, irresistible and hideous, freakish and generic, true and absurd. Yet of all the men I have asked, 'Would you like to have met him?' – and this includes several academics who have dedicated years of their lives to annotating and critiquing his thought – none has ever said, 'Yes. Of course.' Most of them have given me a look expressive of something between distaste and terror. I think this reaction is most likely something to do with Foucault's homosexuality: men who unhesitatingly grant Foucault daily admission into their mind's inner sanctum are obsessed with the thought that, in return, in person, he would have demanded a singular admission to the outer chamber of their rectum.*

### 26

It was a small human foetus.

It was suspended in formaldehyde, in a cylindrical glass specimen jar, in an upright position, in a single strong beam of sunlight.

But what was most interesting about this *particular* foetus was that, through some genetic or other abnormality, the two bony hemispheres of its skull had failed completely to enclose its brain.

The formaldehyde had bleached most of the colour from the foetus, but the brain tissue retained something of its original pinkiness. I remembered seeing – once, somewhere – the intestines of a half-dissected laboratory rat which had been fed on nothing but milk of magnesia.

I picked up the specimen jar and carried it to the window for a closer look – my back, facing the arch; my face, to the light.

I thought, for some reason, that there was a chance I might join the foetus in its formaldehyde – that we might have an interesting conversation.

I was about to try prising open the jar for this purpose when Foucault walked in behind me.

### 27

*'Shh,' I said, 'I'm asleep. I'm dreaming.'*
   *'What are you dreaming about?' asked Vita.*
   *'Michel Foucault, the great French philosopher.'*
   *'And?'*

### 28

'Ah,' he said, 'I see you've found Pinky and Perky.'
   'Which is which?' I asked, without turning round.
   'Guess,' said Foucault.

I did eeny-meeny-miney-moe and got the wrong answer.

'Damn,' I said, still pulling at the jar's lid.

I heard a mouselike squeak behind me.

Turning round, I looked.

29

'Well, there's a skull called Pinky and a foetus called Perky.'

'Are you sure it's not a nightmare?' asked Vita.

'I wouldn't know. I've never really worked out what makes a nightmare different from a dream.'

'Nightmares are dreams which have spiders in,' Vita said, definitively.

'So our bathtub, yesterday morning, was a nightmare?'

'Yes.'

'Which is why you screamed?'

'Not very loud.'

'So nightmares are also dreams which make you scream.'

'But the spiders are more important.'

'Then this isn't a nightmare.'

'Do you want me to wake you up anyway?' asked Vita.

'Shh,' I said.

30

A long black leather coat draped down almost to the floor; beneath it lay a body-forming black leather catsuit, covered in obscurely and obscenely placed zips; the feet wore a pair of very heavy-duty black leather motorcycle boots; the head wore an all-over black leather discipline hood, covering everything but the eyes, the ears, the nostrils and the mouth — all of which could be zipped over in an instant.

I could tell this was Foucault, but only because his pale skin and blue eyes were both still visible — just — through the black shadows of the holes, between the silver teeth of the zips.

The mouse squeak I'd heard, and which had made me turn, was Foucault's knees, kissing.

He looked like an evil superhero — like someone Captain America or The Silver Surfer or Superman or The Human Torch might be called upon to do battle with.

But, then again, he also looked like the perverse hermaphrodite outcome of an illicit union between Batman and Catwoman.

He walked from the doorway to the desk. Put down two tumblers of a clear ice-cubed liquid. Held out his hands. Smiled. Took the specimen jar from me. Placed it back in its original position on the desk. Adjusted it. Smiled.

'Here,' he said, passing me one of the tumblers.

He watched as I took a sip and then knocked his back.

'What does it taste of?' he asked.

'Hummingbird,' I replied.

'Interesting,' said Foucault. 'And mine tastes of Algeria.'

'Sounds a bit dry,' I said.

'Let's go,' he said. 'We're late.'

31

*'Are you sure you don't want me to wake you up?' asked Vita,*
*after I had described Foucault to her. 'He sounds scary. He*
*might rape you.'*

*'No, I'm fine. I want to see what happens. Wake me up if I*
*start screaming.'*

32

As we spun down the spiral staircase, I tried to catch a
glimpse of the slogan on Foucault's badge. But Foucault
was ahead of me, skipping down the stairs – a blur, a bat,
a man, a soul. His badge was indecipherable.

(I had worked out some of the system of this particular
dream. The badges were clues. By their slogans and
colours, they gave hints as to what was going on and what
was coming up. The hints weren't very clear, but they
were better than nothing. The tastes of the drinks, on the
other hand, as far as I could see, were meaningless.)

I looked down at my own badge, wondering why I
hadn't done so before. The slogan, red on yellow, read:

DANTE

When we got into the convertible, back in the heat of
San Francisco, I was able to confirm that Foucault's
slogan, red on green, was:

'Therefore I'm going to hell,' I said. Or thought. Or thought I said. Or didn't.

### 33

*'What?' said Vita. 'Tell me what's happening. I want to know.'*

*'I'll tell you in the morning,' I said.*

*'But you'll have forgotten by then.'*

*'Go to sleep,' I said. 'Please. I'm trying to concentrate.'*

### 34

Whilst we were in Foucault's apartment, night had fallen. The sky was still pinkish at its peripheries, but overhead was inky blue muzzed with streetlight yellow.

The Thunderbird was where we had left it.

Foucault picked up a pair of welding goggles from the back seat. Someone had obviously stolen the driving goggles and left these in their place. Without comment, Foucault took off his spectacles and put the welding goggles on.

We drove off. I lay back in the receptive leather of the seat, looking up. My hummingbird-on-the-rocks was taking effect.

In the pulses between streetlights, the moments of rhythmic almost-dark, the stars faded briefly into focus.

For some reason, it seemed to me as if each of the stars was no longer a point but a line – and each of the lines found its origin and destination in me.

When, after half an hour or so of stargazing, I looked down at the road, I thought Foucault had driven us into a funfair or a firefight.

Lines of wavy blue and red neon ran for block after block. Streetlights were blazing auroras. People walking along the sidewalks, lighting cigarettes, weren't using matches but hand grenades. Yellow pervaded everything.

I realized now why Foucault had so willingly donned the welding goggles.

I closed my eyes and found that I had a picture of the devil tattooed on my eyelids. Only it wasn't a picture. It smiled.

I opened my eyes and looked at Foucault. Onto the dome of his forehead were projected stripes and dots and arrows and words. He was looking at me, smiling. Carnivorously. He had removed the welding goggles but had not put his spectacles back on.

I noticed that the automobile had stopped.

'We're here,' he said.

'Where?'

'You'll see,' he said, and pointed through the windscreen. I turned to look.

### 35

*I noticed that Vita had turned away from me, onto her side, as she does when she is serious about getting to sleep.*

### 36

We were in a drive-in movie theatre. It took me about an hour to work that out. Before then I thought we were:

- in a tropical paradise
- in hell
- in a silver, white, pink and red Thunderbird convertible
- in a film studio

I couldn't figure out what sort of movie we were watching. It was in colour, of that I was certain: in fact, it was in some new kind of ultra-Technicolor.

The colours were so vivid and exhilarating, so symbolic and vast, that they completely blotted out the dialogue and the actors.

The plot, when you saw it thus, reduced to its essentials, was the age-old battle between Red and Green. Red tended to occupy the left half of the screen, Green the right. As always, I sided with Green – yet for long periods, Red was in the majority. This temporary triumph was celebrated by the rasps and raspberries, brayings and neighings of a battery of wind instruments. While they blasted, I felt like I was being pushed closer and closer to a furnace. At one great climactic chord, I felt my eyelashes being singed and afterward smelt the acrid remains of my nostril hairs.

But then, for brief intervals, Green would somehow come to pervade – taking over the whole screen: a dominance Red never quite achieved.

Green's victories were always acquired by seeping slyly in from the peripheries, never from a full-on assault. At these moments, I exulted in what felt like a personal victory. Green's screen-domination was celebrated by watery sounds from the strings, from trickly ripples to great crashy breakers. Often they were quiet, mimicking the pleasant lull of distant oceans. But then, at awful moments, the whole string section crashed down on top of me – wave after triumphal wave, threatening death by sonic drowning.

At the lowest point of my submersion, I opened my eyes and saw a mermaid, Vita, sleeping, lovely.

I thought I was dying.

Then, suddenly, a new presence was on the screen. Black with white lines floating upwards. I was tumbled up onto a final beach. There was a great reconciliation achieved between strings and wind. There was resolution of colour into non-colour and total colour. There was synthesis. There was peace.

I found that I was crying.

I looked across at Foucault, who was scraping popcorn from an almost-empty carton. His blue eyes were looking at me.

'What do your tears taste of?' he asked.

I took one of them on the tip of my finger and put it on the tip of my tongue.

'Three,' I said.

'In the morning?'

'In the morning,' I said. 'Why, what do yours taste of?'

'Burnt umber,' he said.

'Sounds a bit — '

I lost consciousness.

## 37

*When I lie in bed at night, unable to fall asleep, I often half-open my eyes. Because we live in the city, Vita and I, there is always light. Over the past few years, the curtains in the bedroom have become steadily thicker — in a vain attempt to preserve and extend, to deepen and darken the Sunday morning lie-in: net curtains, white curtains, patterned curtains, lined curtains. But always, light from the streetlights — light reflected back off the clouds in the sky and the leaves of the trees, the walls of other buildings and the minerals in the tarmac — light manages, somehow. Through half-open eyes, there are always the two diagonal bars of muzzy greyish, greenish, brownish, reddish light — dripping off the bottom edge of the curtains or seeping over the gathers at the top.*

## 38

When I woke up again, we were no longer in the drive-in movie theatre. I couldn't see where we were: it was dark but there were lights nearby. We weren't moving.

I heard Foucault's costume squeak against the Thunderbird's leather seats. Nothing of him was visible except for two pale rings: the white skin surrounding his

sunken eyes. Ghost-doughnuts in the wardrobe-dark.
No glasses.

'Are you awake?' he asked.

'Yes.'

'Come on then,' he said. 'Let's go.'

'No!' I said. 'Can't we talk about philosophy? I've
always wanted to meet you.'

'Why should we talk about philosophy when we can
so easily practise it? We are about to enter a philo-
sophical laboratory: to investigate the hermeneutics of
pleasure, to become archaeologists of the subject, to
reconstitute an erotics of truth, to challenge the *episteme*
face to face. Either you come or I leave you here.'

I got out of the car, feeling light but clear-headed.
I tripped over something. Foucault took my hand and
led me round the corner.

Immediately in front of us was a long alley at the end
of which was a bonfire of red neon.

As we approached, I was able to read the word that
was written in bloody fire. The word was *hell*.

## 39

*I got out of bed and edged my way into the kitchen. Without
turning the light on, I poured myself a glass of water and drank
it. Then I went through into my study and sat down on my
black leather armchair. The light through the net curtains reflected upon the spines of my books. I stood up, reached up.
My fingers felt.*

## 40

We walked up to the front door, under the neon and into a small foyer containing a cashier's booth. As I knew it would, a sign said, 'Abandon all hope, ye who enter.' But another sign beneath it said, 'Cover Charge: $1.50.' Foucault paid.

Through some plush red velvet curtains, down a long black painted flight of stairs, through some more plush red velvet curtains, into hell.

Hell, to my surprise, was non-smoking.

We walked over to the bar.

'I'll have a Bud,' I said.

'Two Buds,' said Foucault, to the barman, who was not Barman–Nietzsche.

I looked around the bar. There was a lot of leather and a lot of rubber. The rubber was tending to gather on the right side of the room, the leather on the left. On the far wall were four doors through which, at intervals, rubber and leather wandered in and out. When a door opened, the music and the screams got louder; when a door closed, they were almost inaudible again.

Our drinks arrived and I relaxed enough to speak:

'Michel, shouldn't I be wearing stuff like that?'

'Your badge is very S/M, Toby. It's quite enough.' I looked at my badge. In purple on yellow, the slogan read:

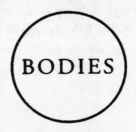

I looked at Foucault's badge, but he'd covered it over with his hand.

'What do you think it says?' he asked.

I knew but I didn't want to say.

'"Buildings"?' I pretended to guess.

'No.'

'"Minds"?'

'No.'

'I don't know.'

Foucault's badge, when he revealed it, bore the expected slogan, in black on red:

PLEASURES

'Do you want to explore? See what's going on in the other rooms?'

'No,' I said. 'I really don't want to. No.'

'Come on. It'll be fun. It'll be cool.'

'No.'

'What does your drink taste of?'

I tasted it.

'*Paradise Lost* by John Milton. Why, what does yours taste of?'

'Mine tastes of Maoism.'

'Sounds – '

'You said,' said Foucault.

' – wet.'

There was no one in the bar but men. The room was dark. The men were talking. The men were wearing a lot of leather and a lot of rubber. The men were talking about rubber and leather. The men were wearing a lot of leather and a lot of rubber. The men were talking. The room was dark. There was no one in the bar but men.

Loud music was playing in the other rooms, but it didn't quite cover the screams. The screams from the other rooms were just audible over then the music.

I tried to hang onto these things.

Our badges changed. I watched them do it.

Foucault's badge, again white on black, again read:

Mine (yellow on purple) read:

41

*My fingers moved over the spines of my books: Eribon, Macey,*
*Miller, Foucault.*

42

'Well, stay here then. Because *I'm* going even if *you're*
not. It's what I'm here for.'

I stalled.

'Come on,' said Foucault. 'This is the end.'

'No. No, thank you. I'm fine here.'

'Come on'.

Foucault left me alone in the room. The room which
was dark.

Foucault went through one of the doors. The second
from left.

Foucault walked into the music and the screams. The
door shut.

The men were talking about rubber and leather.

Foucault was gone. I became very conscious of my
breathing, as if I were wearing a discipline hood.

I followed Foucault. I went through the same door.

The corridor was very dark. The music was louder.
The screams were louder. It was a labyrinth. I stepped
forward. Bumped into walls. Turned left. Turned right.
Turned right. Turned left. The music was quieter. The
screams were louder. There was an alcove. The alcove was
very dark. Hands were on my body. Undoing my belt.

'Michel,' I said. 'Stop that.'

Pulling down my trousers.

'Mmm,' said a voice in my ear. 'Denim. Very kinky.'

'Michel?'

'I'm sorry,' said the voice, which sounded very familiar. 'My name's not Michelle. Is she a friend of yours?'

'Vita?' I asked. 'Vita? Is that you?'

### 43

*I sat back down with what I was sure was my copy of
Foucault's* Discipline and Punish *(London: Routledge,
1977). I opened it up halfway through and looked at the white
space crossed by black lines.*

### 44

'Don't talk,' said the voice, which I was sure was Vita's.
'We don't like giving names here. Call me Michelle if
you want. Call me by a girl's name. I'll call you Vita.
We'll be lesbians.'

'That's not my name,' I said.

Vita's right hand was now gripping my penis. My
penis was erect. With her other hand, she took my hand
and guided it onto her penis. Her penis was erect. I
reached up with my other hand to where her breasts
should have been. They weren't there. In a panic, I
grabbed at my own chest. To my relief, it was still flat.

'Vita?'

'That's *your* name.'

'Are you a man or a woman?' I asked.

'What do you want?' the voice said.

'I want to find Michel.'

'There aren't any women here.'

'So *you* must be a man.'

'Not if you don't want me to be.'

'Am I really in hell?'

'Not really. If you come in the front door, the club's called *heaven*. If you come in the back, the sign says *hell*. But they're the same place. You can choose where you want to be.'

'Do you know where he is? Are you him?'

I reached up, grabbed some of Vita's hair and yanked at it.

'Mmm,' said the voice. 'That's better. I like that.'

Her grip tightened on my penis. I realized that I had not let go of hers. I let go.

Immediately I felt her hands on my head, pushing my face forcefully down her body. Her penis slid into my mouth. I had never done this before. My first thought was that it must be my own penis that I had in my mouth. I had never before been so close to another person's penis. I bit at it, just to make sure. I felt nothing, no pain, but the hands on my head tightened their grip and pushed me further down.

'Go on,' she said. 'Bite me.'

Her penis was almost at the back of my throat. I had to move my tongue out of the way. It slid over her foreskin.

'Peel me back,' she gasped. 'Go on.'

I still couldn't believe it wasn't my own penis, so I reached my hand up to the shaft and pulled the foreskin gradually back. I felt nothing. Vita shook with pleasure.

'Now suck. Suck me.'

## 45

*I took the book through into the bedroom. Vita was lying there,*
*either asleep or pretending to be asleep. In either case I didn't*
*want to disturb her. I got into bed, laying the book under*
*my pillow.*

## THE END

## 46

When Vita came, I was so startled that I instinctively
swallowed. The residue of sperm on the roof of my
mouth didn't really taste of much. If it tasted of anything, it was the taste of my own mouth, intensified. My
erection was becoming painful.

Vita lay back for a while, breathing. I sat down beside
her in the alcove, tugging up my trousers.

From somewhere not too far away there came a
particularly loud scream. It was Foucault.

I stood up immediately and began to run. I turned
several corners, still doing up my trousers, trying to
approach an increasingly bright light. I felt I had to
rescue him.

In other alcoves, there were other couples. After
several minutes of panic and several more screams, I
entered a small room.

Foucault was hanging, upside down, in the centre of
the room, surrounded by a circle of sixteen men. He was
naked but for the discipline hood covering his head.
He was facing towards the door I had entered by. His
arms were held straight out, but his legs were strapped

together: he was being inverse-crucified. His body was supported by a spider's web of leather straps. There were large silver tit-clamps attached to both his nipples. A row of eight smaller clamps ran along the underside of his penis, which was dangling over his abdomen. It was not erect.

Behind him stood his torturer, dressed as a devil, heating something on a small stove. The circle of men watched, some with their arms folded, some with their arms round one another. The man I had thought was Vita came in from another door. He did not look at me, though he must have recognized me – I was the only man in the room not wearing rubber or leather. I have no idea how I recognized him.

I noticed that Foucault's body was completely hairless: no armpit, pubic, chest or leg hair. His blue eyes looked out at me through their holes. There was a horrible pleading in them.

'Don't speak!' he shouted. 'Don't name me!'

He wriggled furiously in the trap.

'I am nothing but a body! I have no face! I have no sex!'

The torturer stepped away from the stove, holding a glowing poker. The movements of his head were exaggerated by his horns; those of his body, by his tail.

He stepped round into Foucault's line of vision.

Foucault's eyes closed. He was silent.

The torturer applied the poker to the tit-clamp on Foucault's left nipple. As the clamp heated up, I could see the veins and sinews in Foucault's neck rippling with suppression. The torturer then heated the right tit–clamp. Foucault let out a half–animal whimper. His penis became half–erect, then went flaccid.

The torturer moved out of Foucault's sight and began making passes with the poker over the skin of Foucault's back. Not touching but almost touching. Foucault flinched away. His eyes opened then closed. When they were open, they fixed on me.

The torturer came back round to the front. He lifted the poker, ceremonially, then brought it slowly down until it rested along the clamps on Foucault's penis.

Foucault bucked and twisted and shook and tensed as the clamps heated through. But he did not scream.

The men watched, in silence, with a sort of deep connoisseurship – as if they were matadors lined up to watch a bullfight.

The torturer stepped back into Foucault's direct line of vision. 'What are you?' he asked.

'Nothing, Master,' gasped Foucault. 'I am nothing, Master.'

The torturer laughed. It was a strangely familiar laugh – a sort of half-drowned glottal cooing.

'Wrong,' said the torturer, bringing the poker up to Foucault's face. 'You are one of the guilty.'

'I am one of the guilty, Master. I am one of the guilty, Master.'

'You are a condemned man.'

'I am condemned, Master.'

'You must be punished.'

'I must be punished, Master.'

'You must be tortured.'

'Yes, I must be tortured. Please torture me. Please, Master.'

'No!' said the torturer. 'Someone else must torture you. Someone else in this room. You cannot choose your torturer. You cannot choose your torture. Your will is nothing. You have no will. You are the condemned man. I will choose your torturer. *He* will choose your torture. I will choose – you!'

The torturer pointed directly at me.

'Step forward,' he said. 'This is the condemned man. He must be tortured. Torture him. Make him feel un-utterable pain. Make him suffer for his guilt.'

The torturer handed me the poker. Its end had quietened from a fierce yellow to a sombre red. It felt surprisingly light, as if it were made of aluminium.

I stepped over to within a couple of feet of where Foucault was hanging and brought the poker up close to his eyes. They looked up at me, blue and pleading.

'Don't!' he whispered.

'Gentlemen,' I said. 'I know this man.'

'No!' screamed Foucault. 'No! No! No!' He was trying to drown me out. That could not be tolerated.

I turned to the torturer.

'I assume you have a gag,' I said.

The torturer nodded and picked a ball-gag up from behind the stove. Foucault tried to bite me as I went to insert it into his mouth. I twisted one of the tit-clamps to make him comply. He complied.

The room went very quiet when Foucault's screams ceased.

I walked once round Foucault, as I had seen the torturer do, examining his naked flesh, marked with the white scars and green bruises of previous brandings, piercings, clampings, cuttings.

'As I was saying,' I began 'I know who this man is.'

The moment I said this, I knew exactly what I would do. I anticipated it almost as clearly as I would have remembered it, had it actually happened. I was in utter control. The future would happen as I intended, and it would happen like this:

I began by saying: 'This man is Michel Foucault, the famous French philosopher. I will tell you eight facts about him. With each fact I tell you, I will burn a line into his flesh with this poker. Please reheat the poker.'

The spider's web quivered with Foucault's strugglings.

There was a long pause, during which none of the watching men intervened.

The torturer handed me back the poker – whiter, hotter, heavier, fiercer.

I said the following words: 'I have already told you the first fact: This is Michel Foucault, the great French philosopher.'

I burnt the line. Foucault screamed around his ball-gag. The line was a single vertical line.

'Second fact: He is the author of a number of books, including all four volumes of *The History of Sexuality*.' Diagonal line.

By this time the men, including the false-Vita, had all shuffled round to get a view of his back, trying already to decipher the inscription.

'Third: He was born in Poitiers on October 15th, 1926.' Another diagonal. 'Fourth fact: At the age of twenty he gained admission to France's ultra-prestigious École Normale Supérieure.' Another vertical. 'Fifth: In 1961 he received the Doctoratès lettres.' New character: vertical. 'Sixth: In 1969 he was elected to the Collège de France.' Horizontal. 'Seventh: In 1975 he visited California for the first time and discovered the bodies and pleasures of some rather different institutions: S/M, LSD, Fisting, Poppers.' Another horizontal.

I then reached down and began to unzip Foucault's discipline hood. I saw, though the holes, that he was crying. When the hood was fully unzipped, I turned to the audience and said:

'Behold the face of Michel Foucault!'

The hood dropped onto the floor, and, with it, the gag.

Foucault immediately began screaming, in French:

'I'll kill you! I'll kill you!'

I drew a slow circle around the two completed characters – his flesh puckering and fizzing at the poker's touch.

Four lines, now, in a straight-sided W-shape; three like a back-to-front E but with the upper spar missing; a circle encircling the whole: when he was the right way up again, Foucault would have on his back a new and permanent fleshbadge:

I dropped the poker and walked slowly toward the door opposite the one by which I entered. Foucault strained to look at me over his shoulder. His screams quietened as his neck twisted.

'I'll kill you,' he whispered.

'You can't kill me,' I said. 'You're already dead. You died, Monsieur Michel Foucault – and this is the eighth fact – on June 25th 1984, of AIDS-related complications, in the Salpêtrière Hospital, Paris. You were a great philosopher. Your torment was your glory. Goodbye.'

And as I walked out of the club, taking off my badge and dropping it, unread, into the gutter, the sign above the door was *heaven*.